Belief in God in the 20th Century

ISBN: 0-9608440-0-7

Additional copies may be ordered at $3.25 postpaid from:

Ruth R. Elder
c/o 2331 North Dunn Street
Bloomington, Indiana 47401

BELIEF IN GOD
IN THE
20TH CENTURY

BY
JOHN ELDER

Nur-i-Alam Publications
1982

CONTENTS

INTRODUCTION

In many places in the world today the impression has been spread abroad that the advance of modern science has disproved the teachings of religion, and that a reasonable and educated man can no longer hold to a faith in God. Many believe that faith and science are irreconcilable enemies, and that one must choose to follow the one or the other. They feel that either one must accept the facts of life as revealed by science and govern his life accordingly, or he must shut his eyes to the findings of science and blindly follow some ancient creed. Now, if this is the case, there can be little doubt that religion is doomed to decline and disappear. Few modern men, in view of all the achievements of science, are ready to ignore its conclusions. If they must choose one or the other, they will choose to live by science. They will look back on the Middle Ages as being the ages of ignorance and faith, while the twentieth century is the time of science and reason.

But such a choice is not required. A third course is open to us. That is to examine carefully the teachings of religion in the light of our highest reason and discernment, to do what Paul urges the early Christians to do—namely to "prove all things, and hold fast to that which is good" (I Thessalonians 5:21). To weigh whether it is more reasonable to believe that this marvelous intricate world is the product of blind unreasoning chance, or to believe it is the work of a master artisan whom we know as God.

In the following pages our thought is to show the falsity of the idea that science and religion are complete opposites, that the idea that one must follow either the one or the other is totally mistaken. First, we shall be looking at some of the philosophical arguments supporting a faith in God, to test them in the light of modern science and recent discoveries. For recent investigations have placed knowledge and information in our hands which we cannot disregard. Following this discussion we shall be considering, without evasion, two great difficulties and problems of faith—viz., sin with pain and sorrow, and finding how they can be reconciled with the existence of a good God. Following that we shall be considering some of the positive proofs of God's existence, such as the existence of beauty, truth and unselfishness, then the relationship between human needs and the provisions found for meeting those needs, and finally, in that section, the evil effects of atheism and the loss of faith. The section following discusses the most convincing evidence for a belief in God, namely the experience and witnesses of the experts in the field of religion and the effect of faith on the individual's life. Next, we shall consider the fruits of faith in Jesus' teaching on the progress of knowledge and learning, on the care of the sick, the care of the needy and poverty-stricken. Finally, we shall consider the ultimate proof of one's personal experience of fellowship with and the knowledge of God as the most convincing proof for the individual.

We send out this brief booklet with the prayer that many who read it carefully and deeply will discover that faith in God is in no way contrary to reason and science but is the normal and reasonable faith for modern man.

[Editor's note: The reader will find a number of allusions to Iran and Iranian culture. This is because the book was originally written to be translated into Persian for an Iranian readership.]

CHAPTER I

REASONS FOR THE DECLINE OF FAITH TODAY

Today there are many who, for various reasons, wish to investigate and discover whether in truth God exists. In places and countries where fifty, or even twenty, years ago nearly everyone believed in a God or in many gods, large numbers are found today who have turned to atheism and materialism and think that to be the way to truth. There are several reasons for this revolution in belief.

Perhaps the first and most evident reason for the loss of faith in God is the occurrence of two devastating world wars in this twentieth century, and the terrible loss of life they caused. In addition were the sickness, pain, loss and suffering that resulted from these wars that affected millions more. Men contend that if there really is a good God, He would not have allowed such things to happen. A good God would not have permitted his children to massacre each other. Farther on in this booklet we shall discuss the problems of sin and suffering. But at this point we would like to emphasize two points.

First, we cannot think that war is something new in the history of mankind. It is probably true that from the dawn of history to the present age there has not passed a single year in which there have been no wars or fighting. The new element is this, that before the outbreak of World War I mankind had taken such long and rapid steps in technological progress that these conflicts were wider and more devastating than any previous ones had been. But, fundamentally, the occurrence of war was no new thing. If it was possible to believe in God before these wars had occurred, it is equally possible to believe in Him after them.

Secondly, while the occurrence of wars and their accompanying suffering and misery may be a difficulty for those who believe that God causes wars, and even makes war a religious obligation, the situation is quite different for those who hold the opposite view, namely that God has forbidden wars and desires his children to live in peace and brotherhood. The fact that when man rejects God's commands, he creates disasters and suffering for himself and others is certainly not an argument against the existence of God. Quite the contrary It goes to support a belief in God. If there is a God, then disobedience to his commands would be expected to produce misfortune and suffering. So when we see that this is what does happen, that in itself is a strong reason for believing in the reality of God and his commands, rather than a reason for doubting Him. Nevertheless it is true that those wars, with their vast attendant suffering, shook the faith of many and destroyed that of others.

A second reason for loss of faith in the present age is the conflict between the modern scientific discoveries and the teachings which religion had previously given. Young people who have gone to colleges and universities and studied modern science have discovered for the first time the conflicts between the new learning and the old religious teachings. Quite understandably they have accepted the new scientific discoveries and cast their religious faith aside. All the same this rejection of religion may be superficial, hasty, and ill-founded. First one should ascertain whether there is a conflict between the actual principles of science and religion, or whether the conflict is between science and later accretions to religion. For it often has happened that religious leaders, lawyers and commentators have added many traditions and comments that are not to be found in the pure original teachings of the founder of the religion. Such additions and perversions can be cast aside without changing the basic teachings in any way. On the other hand it is to be noted that repeatedly claims made by scholars or scientists as representing the last word of the assured results of science, have been found to be mistaken, or only partly true. So if we have been thinking that religion has been defeated in every apparent conflict between science and religion, we are quite mistaken. In addition, the discovery that science has disproved the claim of some one religion does not by any means invalidate all religions, whose teachings may be and are quite different. Proof that some ideas of God are mistaken does not constitute proof that there is no God. For example, when astronomers proved that the beliefs of the ordinary man in regard to the sun, its size, composition and location were wrong, this did not constitute proof that there is no sun. In the same way the discovery that many ideas regarding God and his activities are mistaken does not constitute proof that there is no God. Nevertheless it is undeniable that many, when they have found that science conflicts with their particular religion, have as a result cast aside all religions and all ideas about God.

A third reason for the abandonment of faith in God is the impression some have that the advances of science are such that man can live by science and no longer needs religion, whatever truth there may or may not be in it. It is not that they feel religion has been disproved so much as it is the belief that science is qualified to meet all of man's needs and solve all his problems, so he no longer needs to turn to religion. And it is undeniable that in many emergencies of life in which previously men turned for assistance to religion, today they turn to science—and they do so because experience convinces them that science does a better job. Formerly, when a mysterious epidemic such as cholera or the plague appeared, which threatened their lives, men and women thronged the churches and mosques and besought God's pardon for their sins and his healing power to save. But today they turn to the departments of public health for the setting up of quarantines and inoculations against the dread disease. Similarly in ancient times, and even today in some places, the farmer's hope was in faith and prayer. But today that same farmer, or his sons, go to a school of agriculture and learn such things as the varieties of soil, seed selection, dry farming, irrigation and the value of farm machinery for doing the heavy work. They return to their farms to raise far more and better crops. In ancient times when going on a journey, travellers depended upon the effect of their prayers and made vows to their gods for their protection. But today they depend on the safety regulations of governments, lighthouses at points of danger, radio information on the weather and the adequacy of lifeboats. These changes ultimately are for the good of both science and religion. Science makes great strides, and religion is freed to devote all its energies to its real goal. Religion's real goal is the development of the spiritual life, the setting forth of ideals of character, aiding men and women to a fuller, richer life. Religion must teach men the truths about God and show men how to find God. It must free men from the slavery of sin in this world and show the way to salvation in this world and the next. Science is primarily concerned with the material, religion with the spiritual. Inasmuch as man's essential being is spiritual, needing strength and guidance and light, and that he has a thirst for God, religion that satisfies these needs will never be superfluous. When all of the physical needs of man have been met, his spiritual needs will still clamor for attention, and only religion is in a position to meet these needs.

Still a fourth reason for the decline of faith is that—probably for the first time in history—several countries are ruled by men who not only deny there is a God but who consider all religion as baseless superstition and that it is their duty to uproot any belief in God. While there are many who feel that Karl Marx's economic views can be separated from his denial of religion, and that one can be a socialist or even a communist in economic changes without opposing religion, the official versions of communism as taught in the communist-dominated countries require warfare against all religion. As a result they have founded anti-God museums, publish anti-religious magazines and books, persecute believers in varying degrees, bar them from high office and exclude their children from important positions, confiscate church buildings and property, forbid their doing social service or inviting others to their faith, and do all in their power to stamp out faith in God. Their theory is that religion is designed to keep deprived people from revolting by promising them happiness in heaven, and that once a socialist state is set up and oppression and deprivation cease, religion will wither on the vine. Much to their surprise this has not happened. An amazing percentage of people still believe in God. Even Stalin's daughter asked for baptism and joined a Christian church. But undoubtedly the impact of ceaseless godless propaganda has been to destroy the faith of many.

The loss of faith which has spread throughout the world has other causes as well. There are, for example, philosophical objections that need to be considered. Another cause is the failure of so many believers in God to live in harmony with their teachings. Their deeds belie their creeds, so men doubt the reality of their creeds. Another difficulty stems from the fact that all men do what is wrong, and since they do not want to be punished for their sins, often welcome a teaching that denies there is any God to punish them. These considerations, and many others like them, demand that those who believe give reasons for their deepest beliefs so that men may understand that not only is faith in God logical and reasonable, but that it is the most logical and most reasonable of all beliefs.

CHAPTER II

TWO PHILOSOPHICAL REASONS FOR A BELIEF IN GOD

First, we must reflect upon the general philosophical reasons for a belief in God, having in mind the often forgotten fact that in the realm of ideas such faith cannot be proved with the logical certainty that is possible in the realm of mathematics or physics. If God is what religion teaches, then it is evident that one should not ask for a material and physical demonstration.

Religion teaches that God is not material, therefore it is unreasonable to demand that we show God to any who wish to see Him, the invisible, in order that one may believe in Him. The most that can be reasonably asked is that we show that belief in God is more reasonable and logical than atheism. If we can show that faith in God is probably true, that is enough to lay on us the duty of acting as though He were true. It may be that at first glance this would seem insufficient grounds for determining our moral and religious obligations, but a little reflection will convince us that in the realm of action and duty we have to base our actions on probabilities rather than absolute certainties.

For example, a child falls ill. If the disease seems to us to be dangerous, we feel that we must take him to a doctor for treatment. But why? Are we able to prove indisputably that the doctor will be able to diagnose the trouble accurately? We only feel that probably he will be able to make a correct diagnosis. Again, can we prove that even if he does rightly diagnose the disease and its cause, he will be able to treat it successfully? Once again we must answer "no" we cannot prove; we can only feel that probably he will be able to do so. Again, even if he is able to diagnose and prescribe successfully, can we prove he will do so? Perhaps he is too tired to bother, or perhaps he does not like me, or children. Still we feel that probably he will do his best. Perhaps he writes out a prescription. Can we prove that the druggist in filling the prescription will be able to read what the doctor has written, or if he does, will not make any mistake in mixing the drugs? Again the answer is no. But the probabilities are that there will be no mistake. In addition to all this, can we be sure that the drug manufacturer has made no mistake, and that the bottles are inerrantly labeled? Certainly not. Yet, despite all these possibilities of error and the impossibility of proving that calling the doctor is a wise step, still we would feel it a sin not to ask a doctor's advice if one is available. We cannot prove that it will have the slightest good result for the child; still, if we failed to avail ourselves of the best resources science has placed at our disposal, we would feel we have been guilty of negligence and that we deserve condemnation and rebuke.

Consider another example. Spring has arrived and the farmer is ready to sow his seed. Everyone will agree that this is his duty, as the land and seed are in his control and he should prepare for the harvest. But are we able to prove to this farmer that if he sows his seed, he will gain a good result as the fruit of his labor? It may be that in carrying out this project he will overtax himself and drop dead. Even if he survives it is possible that such heavy and continuous rains will fall that his seed will rot in the ground and produce no fruit, whereas if he had not sown the seed he could have used it for his family's food, or sold it in the market. On the other hand, it may be that after he has sown the seed, no rain at all will fall so the grain cannot come up. Or perhaps rain comes and it grows, and then swarms of locusts come along and devour all the growing grain. Perhaps a war may break out, and even after he has harvested the grain, the enemy may come and carry it all away. Yet, in spite of all these possibilities and probabilities, still we know that the farmer, on the basis of the probability that he may achieve a good result, is duty bound to sow his seed.

In just about all of man's actions there is this possibility of danger or failure. The expectant mother prepares clothing for the baby that is to be born, even though no one can prove that the baby will be born at the right time, and even if he does, that he will stay alive. A merchant orders a supply of goods, even though he cannot prove that purchasers will be found to buy it, or that he may not lose it all as a result of a bazaar fire or a robbery. Parents send their child to school, even though they cannot prove that he will live long enough to profit by his education. Even if he does live, they cannot prove he will use his education in useful and wholesome activities, rather than in debauchery and crime. And so we see that merely the likelihood that a certain course of action will be useful lays on one an obligation to carry it out.

Religion is in this same class of actions. If it can be shown that there is a strong probability that there is a God who has given certain commandments, then it becomes obligatory for us to obey Him. Then the proof of the soundness of these laws as we shall see hereafter comes from the results of such obedience. The proof of the pudding will be in the eating.

Proofs for the existence of God are of a cumulative nature. By this we mean that several different lines of evidence combine to make a probability much stronger than would be the case if there were but one. Whereas any one might not be enough by itself to be conclusive, when many divergent lines of evidence support that same conclusion, the matter becomes reasonably certain. For example, an expert examines a five pound note to see whether or not it is genuine. How can he tell? The fact that the number 5 appears on it is not sufficient, as many pieces of paper have this number. The correctness of the color and the design also by themselves are not adequate proofs, as they can be—and may have been—forged. What satisfies the expert is that all the various tests yield a satisfactory result. If the paper, its size, the watermark on the paper, the design, the numbers, the colors, the signature and every other test all give satisfactory results, then—and then only—is it accepted as genuine.

The matter we are discussing also is of this type. Such a vast and significant proposition as the existence of a God above and beyond nature can be approached from many different angles and proved or disproved with varying sorts of evidence. If we discover that many differing lines of evidence converge to the support of this one conclusion, then we realize that the proofs are so strong that we cannot reject them.

One of the most widespread and clear lines of evidence is this—that belief in God offers the best explanation for the origin of the physical world. Concerning the origin of the material world, there are three possible explanations. One is that the universe always existed essentially as it is today, with some changes. The second is that the universe began by spontaneous generation at some definite time in the past. The third is that the universe was created by an outside power. Let us look at each of these separately.

First, then, has the material world always existed? Many recent scientific discoveries give a negative reply to this question. First—from the standpoint of heat. There is no question that infinite numbers of suns and stars are extremely hot, and are constantly cooling down. The degree of heat in some of the heavenly bodies seems to us almost incredible. One scientist has given the example that if a cannon ball should be heated to the temperature of the interior of our sun, the light given out would knock down a man fifty miles away. And great numbers of the stars are far hotter than our sun. According to the principles of thermodynamics, any hot object suspended in space constantly gives off heat. These spheres are cooling off steadily, but have no way of recovering the lost heat. The only future which scientists can predict for the world, the sun and stars, is that they will grow progressively colder until life is no longer possible on the planets and all forms of life will forever pass away. In other words, the world began ages ago at an extremely hot temperature and steadily is cooling down. To put it in another way, it is as though the universe was wound up like a watch in the beginning and since then has been slowly running down until the time it stops entirely. From this it appears that the universe began at some definite time and before that there were no stars or worlds. For, while natural laws explain how their heat is dissipated, it has no way by which it can be gathered in again.

Some scientists have come forth with a different theory which has attracted much attention, and that is that in the beginning the present universe was a vast cloud of vapors, stationary and uniform. This, by virtue of the power of gravitation and friction, became heated up and the celestial vapors gradually gathered together in the shape of globules or spheres. But others, by careful calculations, have demonstrated that the heat which would be created in this way would by no means produce the degree of heat which the stars now possess. So this theory is generally abandoned.

But even this theory postulates a beginning time and a certain original condition to which it is impossible to return. For once these vapors have condensed into solids, it is impossible for them to go back to their original condition. The power of gravity is so strong that it is impossible for solid objects to return to a vaporous condition. This impossibility is reinforced by the fact to be discussed hereafter—that the stars and nebulae are constantly getting farther away from each other so have less and less attraction for each other. According to the laws of gravity, the farther apart they are, the less they are affected by the gravitational influence of the others. Thus there is no power that could return solids to a vaporous condition. We observe that the stars began their history with extremely high temperatures and end up with such extreme cold that no life will be possible. Supposing that heatless vapor should warm up, it also would be under the same laws of cooling off with no way of getting warm again, so that an endless series is not possible. The existing material bodies are so constituted that the colder they get the more compact they become, and in the material world there is nothing to bring them back to their original vaporous condition. So there is no self-repeating cycle by which the original vapor can be reproduced. Thus a beginning in a definite time is called for.

A study of radioactive elements leads us to the same conclusion. There are elements in the world that are constantly giving off light and tiny particles known as alpha and beta particles and gamma rays. These are known as radioactive elements and include uranium, plutonium and radium. These elements, by steadily giving off these various emanations, are gradually transformed into other elements. Uranium changes to plutonium, plutonium changes to radium, and radium to lead. Whatever the cause for this change, in every case heavier elements change to lighter ones. There are no elements in the material world which naturally change to heavier ones. It is possible to suppose that in the beginning there was only uranium, or perhaps some still heavier element that has now disappeared. In any case, the matter was at least as heavy as uranium and like uranium, radioactive and unstable. This material slowly changed to lighter materials in accordance with the laws of nature by radiating alpha, beta and gamma rays. But there is no way in nature whereby these lighter elements should change again to heavier.

Thus we may believe that in the beginning there was only one element, whether uranium or some still heavier element which, according to the laws of nature, constantly turned into a lighter element. So we ask how and when did this heaviest matter come into being? We cannot think that it always existed, because it is unstable and changing. It cannot have come from lighter elements, as the entire process of development is toward lighter elements, not toward heavier ones. Therefore, this basic material must have come into being at some definite time in the past. We cannot believe that it always existed. Therefore, it must have been created.

Another line of evidence which also points to the same conclusion comes from a study of the motion of the stars. According to a well known principle of physics, known as the Doppler Principle, whenever waves of sound or waves of light emanate from a source that is approaching the viewer, their length is shortened in proportion to the swiftness of their approach. In the same way when the source of such waves is going away from the viewer, the wave lengths become longer in proportion to the speed of the source. So it becomes possible to discover whether a star, or a constellation of stars, is approaching or going away, and also to measure the rate of speed of the motion. Naturally, the faster the speed involved the more the wave length will be lengthened or shortened as the case may be, depending on whether it is approaching or departing.

The newest and most accurate measurements reveal a very remarkable fact, viz. that the total mass of stars which we call the constellations, or island universes, are rapidly scattering from a centre, and the farther they are from the original centre the greater the speed at which they are flying. It seems that at one time all the elements of the universe were gathered together at this centre, and after that, by some titanic explosion, began to scatter in all directions at tremendous speeds. As Eddington, the distinguished British astronomer, explains it—the universe is like a gigantic soap bubble which a child blows with his bubble pipe. The more he blows, the farther apart are the particles of soap suds. In the same way the stars and nebulae of which the universe is formed, are flying farther and farther apart. And there is no natural power which can draw them back again, as every instant the gravitational force of other nebulae becomes weaker as they fall farther away. From this it is deduced that the matter forming the universe had a definite beginning in time. It may have been thousands of millions of years ago. The number of years is not important. What is important is that here also we have a clear indication that the universe was created at a definite time, and has not always existed. So we see it is far more reasonable and harmonious with the findings of modern science to believe that the universe had a definite beginning in time, than to believe that it always existed.

But we must consider—how did this beginning occur? Either we must say that the world came into being spontaneously, created itself as it were, or that it was brought into being by a higher and greater power. But we know the materials of which the world is made, and of which the stars are made, and we know their properties and possibilities. Basically, the universe is made up of elements that are not alive, such as gold, iron, copper, oxygen, lead, hydrogen and so on. In other words, it is made of the same materials as the rocks and earth around us. This being the case, can we possibly imagine that a rock, which up to that time did not exist, should decide to create itself—having no mind with which to make such a decision or power to carry it out when made? The impossibility of such an event happening is perfectly clear. But it is possible to conceive that an eternal spirit, without beginning or end, should make such a decision and create a universe. We have seen that the material world was not always in existence. Hence we are forced to the conclusion that the source of the material world is an external spiritual power that always existed before He made the worlds, and this is the power we call God.

At this point there are probably some who will say that doubtless the world was created by the laws of nature, so that no god was necessary to create it. Materialists sometimes seize on this idea, as though in some mysterious way, the laws of nature have a real and separate existence of their own outside the material world, and can all by themselves decide to create a world. But this idea is far from reality. The laws of nature have no existence outside the material universe, and a law of nature is not able to think, to plan or to create anything.

Perhaps we can see this more clearly from an example. Most of us, for example, are fond of reading Firdausi's poetry, and take great pleasure in it. We consider him to have been an extraordinary genius with unique mental powers, who has uplifted the soul of the nation of Iran. But suppose someone should come forward to say that we have no right to honor Firdausi and to describe him as a great poet, because all of his poems were written by the laws of poetry and eloquence, and the laws of Persian grammar, not by Firdausi.

The fallacy of this argument is very plain. For if all the laws of grammar and composition are unused by an author, they of themselves in millions of years cannot—and will not—produce a line of poetry. The laws of nature are of the same type, and cannot possibly create a world or even an atom. One may believe that God created the world in accordance with the laws of nature, or rather, decided on the laws by which the natural world should operate. But the laws themselves have no outside existence and no creative powers. The only condition under which the laws of nature should be able to create anything would be for these laws to exist outside the material world and to possess mind and will. But if we attribute these qualities to the laws of nature, we are simply making a god of the laws of nature, or calling God the laws of nature. So we see we cannot attribute the creation to the action of the laws of nature. They have no such reality and power. They are merely descriptions of what normally happens in the world of nature.

Not merely creation as a whole, but also a careful consideration of the details of creation lead us to a faith in God. Consider, for example, the existence of life on this globe of ours. Where did this life come from and how did it originate? The studies and investigations of countless geologists and biologists have concluded that for long ages of time there was no life on this world. Always the lowest layers of rock in point of age, have no signs of life in them at all. It is only in the more recent rock layers that the first signs of life are found, and in still later layers traces of abundant numberless forms of life are found, fossils that show the presence of living organisms. In addition to this, the more ancient layers of rock are found to be of volcanic origin, rocks that were so hot as to have been fluid like water. That is, in early ages this world was an incandescent ball so hot that even rocks were melted. But long before we reach temperatures capable of melting rocks, we reach temperatures that would immediately destroy any form of life to be found in this world. Life did not—and could not—exist amidst such heat. Following that age there were hundreds of millions of years during which this earth slowly cooled before a temperature was reached at which life could survive.

But when this temperature was reached, from where did life come? What was its origin? It must have had one of two origins. Either it emerged by the chance bumping together of atoms, eventually producing the molecules necessary for the simplest forms of life, or it came as an act of creation by an outside power, or God.

In this connection the distinguished French scientist, Lecomte du Nouy, has made most careful scientific investigations to determine whether these basic molecules could have been produced by the chance collocation of atoms in the time between the earth's molten condition and the appearance of the first forms of life. He points out that the basic principle of all so-called laws of nature is statistical probability. He illustrates this law by the action of a gas under pressure. A gas is simply an enormous number of free molecules always in motion, moving at different speeds, and continually hitting each other and striking the sides of the container. The result is that on the average the same number of molecules hit each side of the container so that the pressure is equal on all sides. And this is not merely a theory but is proved by experience. When a gas is confined in a tight space, the pressure is indeed equal on all sides. It is impossible to predict which molecule will hit which side but it is quite possible to predict that the same number will hit each side. Thus there is a calculus of probabilities that is proved correct by countless experiments.

Then he uses the laws of probability to estimate the possibility that the basic molecules that support life should have come into existence by pure chance. These molecules are extremely complex—containing tens of thousands of atoms. Supposing that the atoms in our terrestrial globe are agitated by 500 trillion shakings per second, which corresponds to the order of magnitude of light frequencies, he finds that the time necessary for the development of one such complex single molecule by pure chance is 10^{243} years, i.e., 1 followed by 243 zeros. But the time available is nowhere near that amount. The earth has only existed for two billion years and life appeared about one billion years ago when the earth had cooled, or 1×10^{9} years.

Thus the time necessary for the appearance of even one such molecule is 10^{243} times longer than the available time. Thus the production of even one such molecule in the limited time available is statistically impossible.

But one protein molecule needed to sustain life is useless by itself. Hundreds of millions of identical molecules must be present at the same place and at the same time. But this is quite impossible, according to the laws of chance. So Professor Du Nouy concludes from calculations on the basis of the calculus of pure chance: "We are brought to the conclusion that actually, it is totally impossible to account scientifically for all phenomena pertaining to life, its development and progressive evolution." He also notes that the remarkable discoveries made at the Rockefeller Institute of the crystallizable viruses of virus diseases of rabbits and of tobacco, which have been hailed as bridging the gap between organic and inorganic matter, actually do not alter his conclusions. First because their molecular weights are so high that the probabilities of their emerging by chance is far smaller, and secondly because these substances are not alive but produce only when they come in contact with living matter. The above is, of course, a very brief summary of an elaborate presentation and readers are referred to the book *Human Destiny* (Book I: "The Methods," Part 3), for the complete demonstration.

The above line of evidence relates to the molecules necessary to support life showing that chance cannot account for their development. Then what shall we say as to the appearance of life itself, that mysterious power that draws molecules together, forms cells, has the power of reproduction, assimilation of nourishment and self-repair. From what we have written above, it is evident that life has not always been a feature of our terrestrial world, but that it made its appearance approximately 1 billion years ago.

Until a century ago scientists who did not believe in a creative God attributed the origin of life to what they called "spontaneous generation." They believed that under favorable conditions dead cells would come to life. It was one of the famous Louis Pasteur's achievements to show that they were mistaken. One of Pasteur's contemporaries had demonstrated that when a soup was boiled so that all life was killed, and the bottle in which the soup was enclosed was firmly corked, after an interval of about two weeks the soup would be found to be filled with living germs. Pasteur did not accept this, but believed that the germs had entered through the tiny holes about the cork. So he prepared a similar soup, boiled it, and then entirely sealed the container by melting the glass opening. When this was done the soup remained indefinitely completely sterile with no signs of life.

Then the opposition scientist, without the slightest proof, argued that there was a certain elasticity in the air that was cut off by sealing the jar, and for this reason it failed to generate germs. So Pasteur devised a long undulating tube open to the air at the far end and ending in the bottle at the other. Germs stuck in the lower bends of the tube and failed to reach the soup. Once again the mixture failed to generate germs. By these and other experiments it has become a well established scientific truth that there is no such thing as spontaneous generation, but merely the transmission of life. When the chain of transmission is broken, no life is produced. So once again life seen as the creation of a creator God seems the most reasonable conclusion.

To imagine that the original volcanic rocks and water could produce life and living creatures is to suppose a development contrary to all experience in the realm of nature. For while a living creature may and does reproduce itself, and may also make insensible objects, the reverse never occurs. A man can pass on life to a child or, if he is skilled, he may build a house. But the reverse never happens. A child never gives birth to a grown man, nor does a house manufacture a builder. A bird builds a nest, but a nest never gives birth to a bird. A beaver builds a dam, but no dam ever built a beaver. The elements of this world are well known and their qualities carefully defined. And none has been found that creates life. As has been seen, some are radioactive and emit penetrating but deadly rays. But none of them emits life. Life only comes from life. It is reasonable to suppose that life, which is invisible, intangible, untouchable, emanates from a God who is likewise invisible, intangible and untouchable.

We constantly see living creatures—birds, animals, fish, insects and human beings, but we can never see their most important quality, namely life. When a person dies there is no visible difference in his appearance or weight five seconds before death and five seconds after. Nothing can be observed leaving him at the moment of death. Yet there is a world of difference, the difference between life and death. And when we reflect that this vital force known as life is invisible, then it is only natural that the source of this life, whom we call God, should also be invisible. And just as we cannot prove we are alive by showing the quality in us called life, so we cannot expect to see with our eyes the all-powerful, omnipresent but invisible source of life known as God. How absurd, then, was the statement of the Russian cosmonaut that nowhere in outer space did he see God, just as though the eternal spirit could be seen by physical eyes.

Another of the qualities of this world which has led many thinkers to a conviction of the reality of God as the maker of the universe, is that on every hand we see evidences of an orderly plan interrelated with other parts of creation. If the world had come into existence by blind chance it surely would not have possessed such planning and order. A recent writer has well set forth the force of this proof in the following example.

He asks us to suppose that a stranger to our civilization should happen to find a running watch lying by the wayside, and should pick it up and examine it. He would at once be impressed by the fact that in all its parts and relations he could see proofs of planning and design, because of a large number of distinct portions acting on one another for the accomplishment of a definite purpose. These portions are so planned and arranged as to produce motion, and this motion is so regulated and designed that it indicates the hour of the day. Had these parts been differently arranged, they would not have produced motion, or perhaps would have produced useless and pointless motion.

From this study two conclusions emerge. First, that the watch had a maker who at a definite time and place, and for a definite purpose, designed and made this watch. And secondly, we deduce that this manufacturer understood how it should be made and planned it for the purpose of marking time. Even though we do not know who the maker was, or know anyone capable of making such a watch, or how such a watch could be made, still we would hold to the above conclusions. Indeed they would but increase our admiration for the unknown watchmaker, but they would not shake our conviction that there must be such a craftsman who had produced such an instrument.

If, for example, someone should point out that all parts of the watch operate in accordance with the laws of mechanics we would not feel that he has explained everything about the watch. For when we see that all portions of the watch work together in harmony to achieve one result, namely showing us the time, we are sure that this points to a plan and design. We are aware that the sort of materials used in the watch are only determinative and decisive to a degree in its manufacture, and in addition a clever watchmaker and designer is required so as to make it tell the time.

Now let us suppose that as a result of closer investigation it should become evident that the watch had the remarkable faculty of being able to reproduce itself and that in the course of time it did produce other watches like itself. And suppose that this watch should have a compartment fitted out to make repairs and to produce spare parts when needed, with a machine to put these spare parts in place when needed, would not our impression be greatly deepened? Unquestionably our feeling of admiration and honor to the unknown watchmaker and his skill would be vastly increased. If great skill and ability are necessary in order to manufacture a watch without these qualities, how much more is necessary to provide them. The probability that this watch we are examining was produced by an earlier watch, and it in turn by one still earlier, would not at all diminish our admiration. We would feel that even had the watch come from an earlier one, still the design and plan for the earlier watch was not of its own making, and our belief that at some time and place there was an original watchmaker who started the line of watches and who would not be in the least disturbed. This then is the proof we derive from a watch. The watch shows evidence of thought and planning, hence there must have been a thinker and planner.

The human eye is likewise another example of natural organs revealing thought and planning. Let us consider this important and familiar example. In order that we may see anything it is necessary that a picture or image of the object fall on the back of the eye, called the retina, from which outside impulses reach the brain. The eye is a means to this end, and in some respects is much like a telescope and there are numerous evidences of purpose and planning in the eye which cannot be denied.

First of all, both in the telescope and the eye it is essential that the light rays be refracted. The lens and the eye's vitreous humor, which accomplish this, resemble the lens of a telescope. The various vitreous humors through which the light must pass do not permit the light to be divided up into various colors.

In the second place, the eye must be so arranged that it may clearly see objects at all distances from those close at hand to those miles away. This is made possible by slight changes in the shape of the lens making it slightly more or less convex. In this way the picture of a landscape many miles away is reduced to one centimeter in size on the retina in such a way that objects included in the scene or at least the larger objects such as hills and mountains all are seen in their right places, and we can see the relative sizes, the colors and the location of each. Nevertheless, this is the same eye that can also see a book a few inches away and read it easily.

In addition the eye needs to be so made that it can adjust itself to various degrees of light. This duty is performed by the iris of the eye, which is a kind of curtain, shaped like a ring, that can contract or expand so as to change the pupil of the eye while at the same time retaining its circular shape. So, the eye automatically adjusts itself to varying degrees of light, whether dark as at night or blindingly light as at noon. It is interesting to see how for many, many years even with the eye to guide them, thousands of technicians have worked scores of years to perfect a camera that possesses some of these qualities which are born in the eyes of every living creature.

In addition, the eye can discern objects in different directions and can instantly turn to the right or left, up and down, without moving the head, and the head can, when necessary, turn the eyes to see what is behind. Furthermore, we have been given two eyes, and these are so made that they work in complete harmony with each other; and yet if one is destroyed the other can carry on and tell the brain what it sees.

Recently also scientists have discovered that having two eyes a short distance apart and each therefore seeing objects at a slightly different angle is what makes it possible for us to perceive depth and distance. It is this discovery that made possible the invention of the stereoscope by which we see the same scene photographed from cameras farther apart than are our two eyes, so making distances stand out far more vividly than normal.

And finally, we can better grasp the wonder and the perfection of the eye when we recall that the eyes, with all their marvelous abilities, were fully developed before the child was born. Before birth, when the eyes were developed, there was no conceivable use for them. They were totally useless in the darkness of the womb. They were not developed as a response to light shining on the body, for there was no light. But they were completely formed to meet a need that would occur months in the future. Reflection on this truth reinforces the conviction that the eyes were not formed by the chance hitting together of blind atoms, but were designed by a wise designer to meet man's needs.

All things considered, it is evident that the eye is an organ designed for the purpose of seeing, which reveals the masterly ability of its maker, and so we are impelled to accept the fact that there was an inventor and maker who designed the organ and was aware of its value. Furthermore, we cannot consider the parents to be in the slightest measure responsible for this design. If, for instance, the eye of a child reveals a planner or designer, we cannot consider this plan and design to be a result of the cleverness of the father and mother. The parents never decided on the shape of the lens or the design of the iris and indeed for the most part are quite ignorant as to how it works. Their parents also were in the same condition, and however far back we go we can never discover an original pair who designed and manufactured the eye. There is no explaining the design and we still look for a designer. But the proof is far wider than this, for there are hundreds of thousands of living species, each one of which has eyes adapted to its special needs and each showing clear evidence of design and purpose and pointing to a marvelous designer.

Furthermore, the eye is only one of many hundreds of living organs found in every living body, each in its own way as amazing and as beautifully designed for its purpose as is the eye. A study of the ear, the mouth, the hand, the heart, the nose, the lungs, and so on leads us to the same conclusion. Beyond this we must remember that man is only one of thousands of living creatures found in the realm of nature, every one of which possesses the same evidences of orderly and planned design, some even more astonishing than the eye.

Not merely does a study of each individual organ in a man's body prove the presence of planning and designing in the world, but the harmony to be seen between the various organs of the body is itself another strong proof of such a plan. Not only, for example, is the eye an instrument for seeing but beyond that the eye of each living creature is the sort of eye necessary for its own peculiar kind of life. In order to understand this inner harmony, let us consider the horse to understand how ideally adapted to its form of life each member is. First, let us begin with the eyes. All living animals may be divided into two classes, the hunters and the hunted. The hunting animals, such as the cat, the lion, the fox, the tiger, the leopard and the like live by hunting other animals or birds. The animals which are themselves prey for the hunters, such as the rabbit, the deer, the sheep, and the dove, live on grass and fruits. The horse belongs to this second group.

We must bear in mind that the animals which are prey for other animals need to have their eyes in the side of their heads in such a way that not only can they see ahead in the direction they wish to travel, but also can be watchful toward the back lest other animals take them unaware. On the other hand, the hunting animals need to have their eyes in the front in order to see and pursue their prey. Thus we observe that the horse has large protruding eyes on the sides of the head so that he can always be on guard. In the horse's body, the mouth is far from the eyes. Thus the horse can bury its mouth deep in the grass it is eating and at the same time be watching on all sides.

Similarly, the ears of the horse are long so that they can pick up the slightest sound and are so mobile that the horse can turn them ahead, behind or to either side. In the case of the hunting animals, all is different. Their ears point forward so they can better follow their prey. The horse's nostrils also are on the sides of the head so that they can smell an enemy from any direction. Whereas, in the case of the hunting animal, the nostrils are forward where they can concentrate on the scent of one particular animal and not be disturbed by other scents from the back or sides. Since a horse must run swiftly and for long distances, its nostrils are capable of considerable dilation so that it can breathe in great quantities of air.

Likewise, the horse's teeth are perfectly suited to the kind of food it eats. Its front teeth are even and so close together that it can readily crop the grass from the ground, whereas teeth like those of the lion, sharp and separated, would not be suited to this food. But on the other hand, the lion's teeth are perfectly suited to tearing meat from the bones of a captured animal or bird. The horse's teeth can move up and down and sidewise so that it can perfectly grind up the hay and oats, which are its normal foods, whereas the teeth of the animals that live on meat are not this way and do not need to be. The reason is that they do not grind their food up but swallow large pieces of meat which they can digest as a horse could not.

For this same reason a horse's mouth is wet while a hunting animal's mouth is dry. The moisture is necessary for digesting grasses and hastens their absorption. Furthermore, the lips of the horse are firm and close tightly so as to hold the chewed-up grasses in the mouth, while the lips of the hunting animals are soft and weak. The horse's feet are perfectly designed for running long distances over hard ground and the horse's hoof is perfectly designed for this purpose. In short, every portion of a horse's body is suitable and adapted to its needs and in harmony with its style of life.

Now we may ask the question—if all of these organs and parts of the body had come into being purely by chance, would there have been such complete harmony and adaptation to the body's needs? If these had each developed purely on the basis of chance, surely all sorts of discrepancies and unsuitable combinations would have emerged; a horse's foot with a tiger's teeth, the digestion of carnivores with the teeth of a grass eater, the eye of a hunter with the ears of one hunted. If the origin of all these forms of life were the result of pure chance, it would be impossible for all of the particular qualities of every animal to be completely harmonious and suitable to its form of life. Rather, unsuitability, malfunctioning, and contradictory elements would be found everywhere. But the harmony which we have seen between the needs of the horse and the adaptation of the horse's members to these needs, is found not only in the horse but in every living creature. From the tip of the nose to the end of the tail every living creature is so created as to produce a complete harmony with its needs and manner of life, and the environment in which it lives.

Therefore, in considering the above facts, we draw this conclusion: that in the natural world there are countless objects and organs, such as the eye, the study of which reveals clearly the presence of planning and design in their origin. Beyond this the unity in the natural world and the way in which each portion interacts with other portions is highly significant. The eye would be useless were it not for light, the ear would have no function were there no sound, the digestive system would be useless without the presence of food. A bee needs a flower as a source of its honey and the flower needs the bee to spread its pollen to other flowers. All of what we call the natural world is filled with such relationships, each meeting the needs of others. Only in recent years has man realized the importance of these relationships in maintaining what is called the balance of nature. Ecology, or the science of the relationship between living creatures and their environment, is fast becoming one of the most vital branches of biological science, as man learns the danger of upsetting this balance by manmade changes. Each revelation of the exactness of this balance is a new revelation of the wisdom and design of the master designer we know as God.

CHAPTER III

TWO GREAT DIFFICULTIES IN HAVING FAITH IN GOD

At this point it is necessary to turn aside for a time to consider two powerful objections to a belief in a wise and good God, objections which constantly bring uncertainty and disturbance to honest thinkers. Because of these two difficulties a great number consider faith in God outside the realm of possibility. These two difficulties are the presence of sin everywhere in the world, on the one hand, and the universality of pain and sorrow on the other. It is probably true that the presence of these two elements in life, more than anything else, has caused man to doubt the reality of God. If God has brought everything into existence and possesses the skill and wisdom required for such a vast work, from whence comes the staggering amount of sin and suffering that are prevalent throughout the world? We echo the thought of a well-known atheist who, when asked had he been creator what would he have created differently, replied he would have made a world without sin. And not only atheists but many believers also are baffled by this mystery. How can we answer this question? If there is a God, why did He not make a world free of sin? And why does he allow the torturing presence of pain?

First of all we must face the fact that our knowledge and experience are very limited. For example, a horse, because of the vast difference between his knowledge and understanding and that of his master, and because his master has plans and responsibilities far beyond the comprehension of the horse, is quite unable to fathom the reason for many of his master's actions. In the same way, and to a vastly greater degree, our wisdom is limited and insignificant compared to the wisdom of God, and God must possess plans and purposes beyond anything that we can imagine. In addition, we must also remember that the universe, the world, and God's ultimate purpose for it have not come to completion as yet, and until it has reached its goal we are in no position to pass judgment on its wisdom or effectiveness. When someone goes past a partially completed building he will see many arrangements there which seem meaningless and deserving of criticism. Some rooms may seem far too big and others far too small; it will seem to him that piles of brick and stones are scattered about without plan or reason; he may find it impossible to discern what is the function of bars of lead, steel or iron piled up at the side. But if he should see that house after its completion, much that was mysterious becomes plain and his criticisms are seen to be baseless. He sees that there was a definite place for each object in the overall plan and that the plan was good. So it is with the world in which we live. The divine purposes of God by degrees are being fulfilled but have not yet reached their ultimate fulfillment. Undoubtedly, when the grand and perfect design of the Creator reaches its completion, many of those very things that seem obscure and baffling to us now will then be perfectly clear and entirely good. We must wait and see.

The Problem of Sin

Even though our science and information are limited and our thinking inadequate, still there is much that can be said in answer to the question: "Why did not God make the world without sin?" First, there is the answer that in fact God did do just that, He did make the world without sin. If we accept the estimates of the astronomers, over a thousand million years passed, after the origin of the world, during which there was no sin anywhere in this world. The sun rose and set upon a lifeless world in which there were no sins or transgressions. Spring and summer, fall and winter came and went and there was no one who broke the laws of God. Nature blindly obeyed every law of God and there was no mind in which the idea of sinning had taken lodgement. If, for example, we should think of the age of this world to be one day of 24 hours, then we should realize that during 23 hours, 59 minutes, and 20 seconds there was no sin in the world; it was only during the last 40 seconds of its existence that sin was to be found anywhere in the world. This being the case, where did sin come from, and why did it appear?

It is obvious that sin appeared on the earth after the creation of mankind, and that there was no sin before that. Even today if there were no human beings in the world there would be no sin. Why is this the case? The reason is that man alone in all creation has been given freedom of choice, and he alone is able to do good deeds or evil, and has freedom of action.

In the inanimate world, the commission of sin is impossible. The raindrops are unable to break the laws or arrangements of God. These drops are formed in accordance with the laws of God and in harmony with those laws fall to the earth and are scattered in all directions by the wind and storms without being able to hinder their own formation or actions. Trees and flowers are incapable of sinning. We sometimes speak of a tree as being good or bad, but all we are saying is that it is suited or not suited to some purpose of ours. A tree cannot be good or bad in the sense of having a fine or an evil character, because the tree has no choice in the matter. The influence of the wind, the rains, the weather, insects and the type of soil it grows in is considerable, and the care given by the gardener also helps; or, perhaps overshadowed by other trees, it is choked out. But in no one of these factors does the tree have any choice whatsoever. Everything is determined for it. Animals also are obedient to their animal instincts which they cannot possibly escape. Fear and anger, sexual urges, and changes in the environment rule their lives. They experience no moral scruples and they are unable to distinguish between good and evil.

It is only when we come to the species of animal known as man that we encounter creatures with freedom of choice who have a moral sense within them. One of the main reasons for man's superiority over the animals is the possession of this faculty, the ability and freedom to choose between good and evil. But it is solely because of this freedom that man can and does commit sins. So far as we can see and understand God could either refrain from creating human beings at all or else create them with this freedom of choice, and hence with the ability to sin. Man without freedom of choice would be no different from an animal, and would not be a human being.

Now, it is possible that some may say: "Could not God have created man free, but in such a way that he could not do anything wrong?" The answer to this is no. If man is to be really free, he must be free to reject the commandments of God or to accept them. But if he is thus free, the time will come when he refuses to accept the will of God, preferring his own desires, and so be guilty of sin. On the other hand, if he is compelled to act according to the will and commands of God, he is no longer a man, but merely a machine. He has become a puppet in a divine puppet show, with God working the strings. In short, God had either to leave the world without any human life, and so free from sin, or to create man with his moral freedom and the ability to sin against his Creator.

Some may say: "If man sins as a result of possessing freedom, is this liberty and freedom of choice worth having?" But when we look more closely at the advantages and benefits which accrue to mankind as a result of this freedom, we can see why it is that God has given this gift to mankind. Because we find that all of the best and finest features of human life derive from the fact that man has been created free.

Freedom is the basis of goodness, the highest excellence of mankind. We take pride in the lives of heroes and saints, who for the sake of serving mankind and elevating the human race preferred pain and struggle to selfish ease, and fame; we take pride in the story of the life of David Livingstone, who endured separation from his family, surrendered ease and comfort, his health, and in the end laid down his life in order that he might serve the black men of Africa. We glory in the courage and valiance of a man like Stephen who, in the early days of Christianity, accepted death with complete dignity and composure; and, refusing to give up his faith, prayed for the forgiveness of those who were killing him. The courage of such men illuminates the pages of human history. The story of the Japanese Toyohiko Kagawa stirs us to the depths, telling how he turned his back on a life of ease and luxury with its opportunities for political advancement and chose to live in the lowest slum of Kobe in order that he might serve his poverty-stricken and unfortunate neighbors more effectively.

But if these men were not from the beginning free in choosing what they should do, then what reason is there for praising them and taking pride in their sacrifices? If they were merely puppets, compelled to do whatever they did by the god who made them, having no more choice in the matter of how they should live than a raindrop has a choice as to where it shall fall, then they cannot be called good, or their actions praiseworthy. So we see that any sort of goodness, courage and heroism, sacrifice and service, and whatever is highest and best in human life, comes from this fact that man was created free and given freedom of choice. Therefore, freedom is probably the highest and most precious quality of the human race.

This being the case, is it not true that should God give man the choice of giving up all of his freedom and choices and living in a sinless world, or of retaining his freedom of choice and decision but living in a world plagued by sin, every man worthy of the name would choose life just the way it is? If freedom is so precious that the finest spirits of the human race have preferred death to its loss, then does it not follow that no one would desire a life like that to continue, denied all freedom. Why should we complain of God's permitting man to sin when this is the inevitable result of giving him freedom of choice; when man himself, if given the choice between a sinless world with loss of liberty and a world of freedom with resultant sin, would certainly choose the latter.

Nevertheless, if it were possible to suppose that God himself desires man to sin—this would create another logical difficulty. If God had planned for human life in such a way that he was not merely able to sin but compelled to sin, and there was no way of escape, then in truth the guilt for sin would be God's, and the fact of sin would be a strong argument against the existence of God.

Here we must face the fact that not all of the beliefs and teachings about God are true, and not every religion gives a satisfactory and acceptable explanation of this problem. There are religions that teach that God leads astray whomever He desires, and rightly guides whomever He wishes, and that He has breathed the desire to sin into every evil man. And if we are compelled to choose one of two explanations and to believe either that God is the source of all evil and sin is in accordance with His will, or to deny the very existence of God, many will prefer to deny God altogether. They will think it better to believe that there is no God than to believe that there is a God who desires evil and leads mankind into sin. But the Gospel teaches us that "it is not the will of your Father which is in Heaven that one of these little ones should perish" (Matthew 18:14). And God in many places commands men to repent of their sins and to come to Him. In the Epistle of James we read: "Let no one say when he is tempted: 'I am tempted by God' for God cannot be tempted with evil and He, Himself, tempts no one" (James 1:13). Thus we see that God not only does not desire man to sin, but is always and everywhere opposed to sin and wants man to flee all manner of sin, and when he has sinned, wants him to repent.

If we wish to argue that God does not will that man should sin, but that when he does sin, God is indifferent and unconcerned, and makes no effort to draw man back to Himself, then to a degree at least the objection is valid. But we read in the Gospels in this regard that God is deeply concerned and offended by our sin and has taken our sins upon Himself. Just as a good shepherd, so long as one of his sheep is lost in the mountains cannot rest at ease in the sheepfold, so God has drawn near us in Christ and has come to seek his lost sheep and suffer for them. And just as a father of a wayward son yearns for his son's return, and when he comes back, receives him with love and joy, just so—Jesus teaches—does God desire the lost to come back home. And so "there is joy in the presence of the angels of God over one sinner that repents" (Luke 15:7). And since Jesus tells us: "Whoever has seen me has seen the Father" (John 14:9), we understand that his endurance of suffering on the cross for our sins is a perfect image of how the Father also enters in our sin and suffering.

Thus, it is evident that the view of God concerning our sins is the same as that of a perfect loving father. Before a father begets a son, he knows that since that son will have freedom of choice in a world full of temptations beyond question, he will at times sin. But despite this due to his fatherly love and also because he is sure that his son will do many and more good deeds, he desires to bring him into the world. In spite of all this, every worthy father is hurt by every sin his son commits, and at the same time that he loves his son and desires his repentance, he hates the sin that his son has committed with all his heart.

In this way we see that sin is inseparable from freedom, and yet this freedom is the most precious of many qualities given by God and a quality which man would not willingly surrender. And we see that not only does God not desire man to sin but is completely and unalterably opposed to that sin, and as a result of that sin he is distressed and suffers that sin may be overcome.

THE PROBLEM OF PAIN AND SUFFERING

We mentioned above that another difficulty in our believing that the world was created by God is the presence of pain and suffering. In some respects this difficulty is even greater than the problem caused by the presence of sin. First it is more difficult because sin is the result of a man's own deliberate decision which he makes of his own free will, whereas the endurance of pain and sorrow is usually not a matter of choice. And secondly, sin is confined to the human race and only appears when man freely chooses it, whereas pain and suffering are found among the animals also, who have no freedom of choice or ability to avoid it. And it is on this account that this difficulty is so great. Why in a world which a kind God has made should there be so much pain and suffering? Even though it is impossible to solve this problem completely, still there are many considerations which diminish its importance and weaken its force.

First of all we must remember that at all times comfort and happiness are far more common in the world than pain and suffering. The vast majority of the human race prefer life to death. If it were not so, they would have committed suicide long ago. The times when an individual endures pain and undergoes suffering are the unusual and exceptional times. There are many people who do not know the meaning of sickness or pain in their own lives, and there are few indeed who always suffer pain. It is the same in the animal world.

Secondly, the intensity of pain as a result of the accidents that happen to men and animals is much less than we usually suppose. The nerves of animals are not nearly so sensitive as the nerves of humankind and many times when we suppose that an animal is suffering great pain, it actually is experiencing no pain at all. For instance, it has been noted that a small crab continues to eat with apparent enjoyment while a larger crab is tearing off its legs one at a time and finally swallows the smaller animal. It was evident that the smaller crab was experiencing no discomfort whatever, otherwise it would have struggled to get away, and not remained there enjoying its meal. Similarly, the great traveler and explorer, David Livingstone, reported that when a lion grasped his shoulder and shook him violently, even though the bone was broken and the flesh of his body badly mangled, at the time he felt no pain at all, as a sort of numbness overtook his whole body. Others like him have reported that at the time when some severe accident occurred they had no sense of pain or discomfort. We naturally suppose that when a cat leaps on a bird and kills it, the bird must be experiencing terrible pain, whereas it may be true that the bird feels no pain whatsoever.

Thirdly, the experience of death which apparently is the most painful of all experiences, actually is rarely accompanied by pain and suffering. Some years ago a writer in the *Atlantic Monthly* discussed the experience of death and claimed that at least five times he had experienced all that goes with death—but each time had escaped the jaws of death and fully recovered. One time he fell wounded on the battlefield, and lost so much blood that he became unconscious. Fortunately, before it was too late, he was picked up, the flow of blood stopped, and he was rescued from death. If help had not arrived in time he certainly would have died there, and as he had lost consciousness, death would not have hurt him in the least. On another occasion he fell down an elevator shaft and immediately lost consciousness. Had it not been for the fact that the elevator was just a few feet below, he would have been killed instantly. And if he had, he would have suffered no more pain or discomfort than he had when he fell and lost consciousness. Three other times he had similar experiences and in each case found that the experience of dying was a painless one, similar to falling asleep. An experienced nurse recently reported that she had been at the bedside of many dying people, and that in each case death came quietly and painlessly. In the vast majority of cases it would seem death is not an experience of great pain or suffering, but rather a quiet falling asleep.

Furthermore, when we reflect on the causes of pain and suffering we find that for the most part they are the natural and inescapable result of God's good laws and arrangements. One of the first of these is the arrangement which we call the rule of natural law. Every event has some cause and every special event produces a certain result. And if this were not so, any organized life on this floating ball we call the earth would be impossible. If the farmer, when he sows a seed, cannot tell whether the crop will be of the same variety or whether it will be something entirely different, there would be no agriculture. If wheat should produce wheat one year, and the next year produce oak trees and the following year poison ivy, there could be no science of farming. Or if the climate in the temperate zone should register 150 degrees Fahrenheit one day and ninety below zero the next, life itself would be impossible. Or if the sun, instead of giving off heat, should attract all heat to itself, there would be no life in this world. And yet we find that the invariable action of the laws of nature lies at the base of most of our pain and disasters.

At one time, as we have seen, the world was a molten mass of hot matter and was perfectly smooth and round. Then as the globe cooled it reached a temperature at which the water vapor became water, and the earth was covered with a smooth coat of water. Had it remained this way, no human life would be possible. But thanks to another natural law whereby all elements shrink as they grow colder, the surface of the earth contracted on cooling, and mountains were formed, like the wrinkles on a drying apple. The emergence of these hills and mountains produced the dry land needed for man's habitation. But this same process is still going on. The earth is still cooling and shrinking, with the result that stresses and strains are set up in the earth, resulting in sudden slippages of the earth's surface in what we call earthquakes. Cracks are opened in the surface, and molten lava pours out, producing volcanoes. These in turn cause great loss of life and property.

We wonder why God allows such loss of life and the damage caused by earthquakes, when in fact the cause is simply the continued operation of beneficent laws without which there could have been no human life at all. We cannot expect natural laws to operate whenever the result pleases us and stop operating when the reverse is true. The foundations of all our science would be destroyed and ordered life impossible, were not these natural laws unchanged and unchanging. All advances and inventions in science and technology depend on the absolute regularity of nature's laws and would otherwise be impossible. And if everyone were given the choice between living in a capricious world, and a world governed by laws, he would undoubtedly prefer the latter, even though this involves dangerous and disastrous experiences such as earthquakes.

A second arrangement which God has made for our happiness and welfare, and yet an arrangement that can cause great unhappiness and suffering, is this: that God has created man a social being, and as a result human beings can influence one another either for good or for bad. A great many of the pains and sorrows which one endures and which are very hard to stand, are the direct result of some mistake or sin of the one who suffers. For instance, it is not hard to understand the pain suffered by a soldier and why this should happen. A soldier entered a battlefield with the purpose of injuring and killing the enemy, but as it happened, he himself was injured. But it is much more difficult to understand the reason for the pain and suffering of thousands of children who have done no wrong, but must endure hunger and nakedness, whose fathers, for reasons they themselves do not understand, were killed on the battlefield in a war they did not start. In the same way it has repeatedly happened that someone living beside a stream has caused a typhoid epidemic. Someone in his family has typhoid and he uses the water of the stream for washing the dishes and clothing of the patient. Farther down the stream others wash their dishes in this contaminated water and perhaps drink the water. As a result hundreds, perhaps thousands, of innocent people contract the disease and die.

Why should this happen? Why should an innocent person suffer illness and perhaps death just because another ignorant, or foolish, or careless, or wicked person does what is wrong? The reason is this, that man is a social animal and so can influence others for good or for evil, and no one lives entirely to himself. Someone may counter: "Then why did God create us as social animals? Why did he not create each one of us separate and independent?" It is true that if He had so created us we would not suffer because of the sins of others, but it is also true that then we would not be able to profit from the goodness and the thinking and the skills of others. When we stop to ponder on how greatly we are indebted to those about us we discover that had God created us in a world where there were no social relationships we would have lost far more than we have gained from our relations with others. There is practically no good thing in our lives for which we are not indebted to others.

If it were not for the help and guidance of others, what sort of food would we eat? We would have had to live on nuts and berries and such meat as we ourselves might be able to kill. If we were alone with no one to teach us it would be impossible for one by himself to discover the secrets of sowing and reaping or making flour and cooking bread. We would have no knowledge of fire, and if we had occasionally seen it in the lightning we would never have thought of using it to cook food. So far as clothes are concerned, we would have to wear a skin from the body of a dead animal or go naked. Similarly, one person by himself would never dream up the idea of building a house, or if he had he would not have had the slightest idea as to how to carry it out. We would not be able to speak, as there would be no one to talk to. Similarly, we would know nothing of reading or writing. Without these advantages we would have possessed almost no valuable knowledge. In addition, all the values of love, education, religion, and the knowledge of God which have come to us, would have escaped us entirely. We would have to get along without all the things that give meaning and value to life. So if man were not a social animal and could not have relationships with others, all of these gifts and blessings would be denied him.

In conclusion, when we examine the matter carefully we come to the realization that if it is possible for man to have social relationships with others, there is bound to be the possibility that he may be injured by their evil habits and actions.

And so we understand that the wicked and evil elements that at first seemed an insoluble riddle are the necessary accompaniments of the blessings and advantages of life—and these advantages are far greater than the disadvantages that inevitably accompany them. Even when we consider the pains and sorrows and loneliness and grief of an orphan child who has come to this state as a result of war and reflect upon it, we see that society has only taken away from the most unfortunate of all of them a portion of what it had previously given. He has lost his home, but he himself had not built that house, society gave it to him. Perhaps the child is almost naked. Still what rags of clothing he does possess, society gave to him, and he could not and cannot produce it for himself. The child is hungry. All the same, he can gather nuts and fruits from the forest just as he would have had to do if he had been born in the forest. Therefore the worst thing that one man can do to another is this: he can take back a portion of what society has previously given. If such disasters happen to an individual, still the individual has gained more than he has lost as a result of his relations with society. He has learned much that he will never forget and that he could have learned in no other way. He possesses life and strength which he could not have found for himself.

And if this is the case with the most unfortunate orphan, it is far more true of the average individual man and woman. I am sure that no one of us would choose to live without the wisdom, comforts, and benefits that come to us by virtue of our relationships with others, even though we would be protected from the injuries they inflict. In other words, if we were allowed to choose between a separate world without any relationships with other men or women, and the world in which we now live with the possibility of discomfort inflicted by others, all of us would prefer the world as it is. And by so doing we would confirm that the present world is right and reasonable, and that pain as an inevitable quality of these arrangements, is not a proof that there is no good God.

In addition to the problem of the pain and suffering which is the necessary consequence of death, and which we have discussed above, the problem of mental anguish, sadness and sorrow must also be considered. Since there is no one in all the world who is always perfectly happy, this problem concerns us all. In studying this it will help to distinguish various basic causes for sorrow in this world. First are the sorrows that come from the nature of things, such as the sorrow and grief for those whom death has taken from us. Secondly is the sorrow and anguish that affects us as a result of others' evil deeds. And thirdly is the sorrow that we cause ourselves by our own sins. The most common cause of grief and sorrow in this world is the constant threat of death. One may perhaps say that more tears have been shed because of the death of our dear ones than for all other reasons combined. And as a result men wonder why there should be such a thing as death.

If we should at this point enter upon a discussion of a life after death and consider the proofs for such a life, we would depart too far from the theme we are discussing. It is enough to say that if, in accordance with the teachings of most religions, there is another and better world, then no one of us would want to remain forever in this world and be deprived of the higher comforts and blessings of that world. If there is such a world, then beyond question we shall be thankful for death that has brought us to that land and we would not willingly return to this world even for an instant. And just as we who are in this world look back upon the life of an unborn child as one of great limitations and would not dream of returning to it, in the same way we shall look at this life after we have entered the other higher life.

But if we look upon death merely from the viewpoint of this world is it not true to say that death is the price we pay for children. If the world were so arranged that children should be born year after year and none should ever die, it would not take long until life would become impossible in this material world. Even with the present limitations on life in most places in the world the population has reached—or nearly reached—the limit of possible support. One of the most common concerns of scientists in recent years is this growing mass of humanity that is being called the population explosion. There are many writers warning us today that such rapid growth in the world's population is terribly dangerous, and we shall soon reach the point where there is mass starvation. If this is the case with man, whose life is in general limited to 70 years, what would have happened long ago had there been no death? Certainly this terrestrial globe would have passed the possibility of sustaining the lives of so many people long ago, and mass starvation would have occurred. Which would we prefer: a stagnant world full of ancient men and women with no children, who might give to life novelty and light and bring hope for the future; or a world such as we now have where the shouts and laughter of little children ring out and the arrival of an army of young people who will carry on after the old have finished their work and passed on brings newness of life? The countless masses of mothers and fathers who have sacrificed their lives and comforts in order that their children might live happily in this world is a sufficient answer. The renewal of life in the world through the birth of a new generation of young people is much more significant and valuable than the tears shed when death comes.

Regarding the grief and sorrow that others impose on us, it is also true, as in the case of pain, that the pleasure and happiness others bring to us are far greater than the grief they cause. There is a very limited number of human beings who wish to live far away from any other persons. Even those few in this age who set off for some distant lonely island far off from mankind are careful to take with them a good supply of the things which civilization has provided such as books, tools, clothing, and supplementary foods, and—for a change—every few years return to civilization and old friends. The happiness and the joy of friendships, friendly rivalry and struggle in this world where human beings live, the mental stimulus that comes from association with others, mental relaxation and spiritual uplift which we find from fellowship with others, these are sources of such happiness that, when we place them beside still other joys that come from those about us, we understand that the griefs and sorrows that come to us through others are relatively insignificant indeed. And when we recall that the pleasures and joys we gain from association with others would be impossible without accompanying griefs and sorrows, then we see that the sorrows that come to us from them are the inescapable effects of provisions that bring us many of our highest and purest joys.

The third cause of grief and sorrow which we must look at briefly is what we find within ourselves. We soon come to realize that these sorrows and periods of sadness are actually a result of our own sins of selfishness and of our making wrong choices. The proof that this is really the case is found in the lives of literally millions of people and the happiness they have found when they have repented of their sins and surrendered themselves to God. It may seem from the outside that their lives are just as before, but the difference is that the same things that once made them sad and unhappy now are an occasion for joy and happiness. In other words, these inner strains and sorrows come from our own transgressions and we lay them on our own shoulders, but when we repent of them we find freedom from our sorrows as well. So this sort of sorrow cannot be a stumbling block for our faith in God but is rather a warning bell that calls us to come to God.

The Benefits of Pain and Sorrow

Until now we have looked on pain and sorrow as completely bad and have shown that even if we suppose that they are entirely bad, still, aided by a faith in God, we can endure them. But when we consider that pain and sorrow also bring benefits and results that are most useful to mankind, then the weight of the difficulty caused by the realities of pain and sorrow is greatly lessened. Let us consider three of these benefits in some detail.

First of all, pain and suffering are warning bells that we may become aware of danger which threatens us, and which are so important that without them it is doubtful whether anyone would reach maturity. For example, some time ago I was the guest of the head man of a small village. When night came we all stretched out on the floor near to an open fire which was gradually dying down. Some hours later a pain in my right foot awakened me, and when I looked I saw that a spark had jumped from the fire and landed on my bedclothes. The bedding had caught fire and spread to my clothes, so I had been awakened by the pain. In a few moments the fire was put out and we went back to sleep. But suppose I had not felt any pain. Almost certainly I would have burned to death and would never have known what happened to me.

In truth there is perhaps no other faculty so vital to the protection of our lives as is the sense of pain. A toothache warns us that the tooth is decaying. If we pay attention and have the tooth filled, we can stop the process of decay and if not the tooth decays and is lost. A pain in the heart warns one that there is something wrong and that he must lead a less strenuous life. If he heeds the warning, he may live many more years. If he does not listen, or if he does not recognize the source of the pain, he will undoubtedly overstrain his weak heart and forfeit his life. The other organs of the body operate in the same way. A pain in any one of them is a signal that something has gone wrong, giving us the opportunity of taking the necessary steps for healing the condition before it is too late.

The second benefit from pain is this: it can and often does produce the finest character. Pain may make a man realize that what he is doing is wrong. Probably all the philosophical proofs or religious teachings will not have half the effect on an irreligious man as will the pain of venereal disease. When one finds he is afflicted with one of these dangerous diseases, no other proof is needed that he has been a sinner and a fool. So it is with intemperance and alcoholism. There are few more terrifying diseases than delirium tremens when the patient believes he is being attacked and overwhelmed by poisonous serpents or ants or scorpions. It is a kind of temporary insanity. Few indeed can experience this horror without resolving to give up the use of alcoholic beverages. Usually they do not carry out their decision because alcohol has already undermined their wills to the point where they have lost their self control. But the horror of this disease, or even the horror of seeing and hearing one afflicted with the disease, is enough to convince anyone of the dangers of alcoholic liquors. The pain and discomfort resulting from smoking opium is similar to this. Usually those who have had the opium habit, and have overcome it, when asked about their experience will tell you much the same thing. They discovered that they were so much under the influence of opium that when the time came to smoke it but there was no opium at hand, they suffered the pains of hell. On this account, for their own protection, they had cast off this burden, and the acute discomfort they endured for a time as a result was the final warning to them of the folly of opium smoking. Thus pain and anguish that we usually look upon as a curse to humanity is often a danger signal which the Creator flashes to warn a man that he is on the wrong path.

Not only do pain and suffering play a vital part in turning men back from wrong and dangerous ways, but enduring them has a positive value in the strengthening and purifying of character, because at the same time they bring new difficulties to life in countless instances, the endurance of pain and suffering brings to the surface hidden strength, and develops feelings of sympathy and courage and endurance. In countless instances the coming of grief, or pain, or sorrow, have resulted in uprooting selfishness and self centeredness from men's hearts and started them thinking about others, and serving mankind.

Some years ago a wealthy couple in American had but one child, a much loved daughter. This daughter contracted scarlet fever and, despite all that the best doctors could do, died of the disease. At first the parents could think of nothing but their own sorrow and loss, but after a time they began to think of others who—like them—had lost a child by this disease, and even more of those parents with children who might one day lose their child by scarlet fever. In the end they gave all of their wealth to a famous hospital in order that they might make a thorough study as to the cause and cure of this disease. The hospital accepted their gift and began their study, and in a few years they were completely successful. Not only did they discover the germ that causes the disease, but they also found an effective cure, and in addition an effective antitoxin by which children can be protected from the disease. As a result it is now possible to eradicate completely this sickness which for so long has threatened the lives of little children. Thus the grief and sorrow of those parents resulted in endless blessings for millions of people.

Many similar instances can be cited. Some years ago an indigent Jewish boy living in Baghdad was given an opportunity to study in the Alliance School. Years later he became one of the wealthiest merchants in the whole Near East, and began to build similar schools in Iraq and all the neighboring countries, so that others might have the same opportunities which were given to him. As a result of his poverty and helplessness, feelings of sympathy and magnanimity emerged that have blessed countless boys and girls.

Some years ago the six children of a Mr. Lee were swept away by a landslide in India, and all of them killed, at a time when the parents were out of the house. Seeing that they had lost their own children, they resolved to become the parents of other children who had become orphans. Today one of the happiest places in all India, where the love of Christ radiates in action, is the Darjeeling Orphanage. Hundreds of children have been given shelter there and aided to physical, mental, moral and religious progress. It was the shock that came to the Lees as a result of their terrible loss that led them into this wonderful service to others. Sympathy is a human quality that is one of the highest and best which we can learn. And the meaning of sympathy is "suffering together." Until one has himself suffered he cannot truly suffer with others. So one may say that undergoing pain and suffering is a necessary condition for nurturing the highest human sensitivities. Even in regard to Jesus Christ, it is written that "he was made perfect through suffering" (Hebrews 2:10).

In the third place it is noteworthy that pain and anguish have contributed so much to the progress of investigation and science that it is difficult to exaggerate their importance. We seldom stop to consider the motives that actuated inventors and discoverers who have led the advance of the human race, but if we investigate the matter we shall see that in nearly every case what impelled them was the desire to avoid pain and discomfort.

For example, consider the inventions and progress in the provision of clothing from the time when our ancestors covered themselves with leaves and grasses up until this twentieth century when thousands of remarkable machines which meet our needs for covering and clothing have been invented and perfected. If one would wish to detail the steps which this development has taken from the beginning, the use of skins, the invention and perfection of tanning and leathermaking, the invention of shoes, and of boots, the discovery of the process of weaving and of dying, the application of steam power to looms, this in itself would fill a book. The invention of and discovery of new textiles— silk, cotton, linen, camel's hair, wool, etc.— would fill another book. Still more could be written about the new artificial plastic materials—nylon, artificial silk, orlon, dacron, and rayon—each with its own value and importance.

This story is a good example of man's conquest of nature and discovery of raw materials that nature has provided. And what has been the reason for these discoveries and inventions? It has been fear of pain and discomfort. Sometimes the goal has been the protection of men from intense heat, sometimes the object has been protection from the cold, or again the protection from chilling rains. It is noteworthy that no inventors of cloth factories have appeared in the torrid zones, but in the colder regions, no matter in what part of the world they may be found, or how primitive the civilization there, the skills of spinning and weaving have been developed to the point where they can meet the needs of the inhabitants. Headaches caused by intense sunlight, chills brought on by cold rains, and the shivering from cold in winter are the basis for the invention and perfections of the arts of spinning and weaving. There would have been no such progress had there been no pain or discomfort.

If this is true regarding clothing, how much more is it pertinent to the provision of foods. Once again, many books could be written about the development of the science of agriculture beginning with the time when primitive man scattered a few seeds on a flat piece of land to the present time when amazing machines plow twenty furrows at a time and sow seed simultaneously. Or starting with the time when the crop was cut with a hand sickle and the sheaves laboriously tied up one by one, until the time when huge reapers cut 20-foot swaths, separate the wheat from the chaff, and pour the grain into efficiently tied-up sacks of equal weight. Books could be written and have been written detailing this progress. This is one of many amazing stories of progress in which mankind can take great pride. Yet all of these forward steps have been taken because of a pain called hunger. The progress in perfecting means of transportation is, in the main, the result of two sorts of pain, pain from the cold and pain from hunger. The large tribes, when winter approached, had to find pasture lands for their flocks and so left the mountains for warmer regions where—in winter—pastureland for their flocks could be found. When there occurred a famine in one part of the country, food had to be transported in from other regions. Cloth that was woven in one city had to be transported to others. In this way man was impelled to develop better and more abundant means of transport and so the way was opened for the perfection of another series of inventions.

It is even more evident that the amazing progress in medicine and surgery is a result of physical pains and diseases. Few institutions in the world can compare with modern hospitals as a source of pride and amazement. With the discovery of anesthetics, extended and delicate operations are being performed daily of which primitive man never dreamed. Entire organs such as the appendix, the gall bladder and an infected kidney are removed daily and the patient quickly restored to health. Kidney transplants are commonplace, many heart transplants have been successfully made. Artificial organs such as artificial hearts and kidneys seem on the point of perfection. Constant exploration in the development of new medicines has released a flood of new and more effective drugs, such that doctors report that nine-tenths of the prescriptions they write today are for medicines unknown ten years ago. But all of these remarkable instruments and machines, all the medicines that are being discovered and developed, medicines that run into the thousands, and all of the amazing skills and methods being perfected, all of these are the result of man's constant fight against pain. So we see that while on the one hand, no one seeks or welcomes pain and suffering, or wishes it to happen to others, yet on the other hand a great part of our progress in invention, science, medicine and technology, progress in which all take pride, is a direct result of the experience of pain. The use and benefits of pain are undeniable.

We have spent a lot of time considering the problems of pain, sin, and suffering because these are always a part of our lives, and are among the greatest difficulties in the way of faith. Let us at this point look back and summarize this section.

First, we considered the problem of sin and recognized the fact that from our limited viewpoint it is impossible to understand all the secrets of life, that as the world's history is slowly unfolding and the history of mankind developing, we have not yet achieved our goals so that we can finally assess the impact of sin. We then noted that the possibility of sinning is a direct consequence of our having freedom of choice, without which man would not be a human being, but a machine or a puppet. Then later we found that this same freedom of choice is the basis for all the virtues and the most precious rights of the race. And finally we saw that God is not indifferent or unconcerned about our pains and sins, but sympathizes with us and takes our infirmities on Himself.

Concerning pain and suffering also we noted that pain and suffering in this world is always much less than its joys and satisfactions, in general and in particular cases. We saw that the animal world suffers comparatively little pain, and that death itself is not usually a pain-filled experience. Next, we looked at the most common causes of pain and suffering and found that there are two of these: first, the rule of law in the natural world without which ordered life would not be possible, and secondly, the friendship and association with other humans, and noted that in return nearly all of the conveniences and comforts we have spring from these same social relationships. On the other hand we saw how pain and suffering play a vital part in human survival and are also most effective factors in the progress of mankind in every respect. In addition they are the most common means for developing man's higher faculties such as love and sympathy. Thus we find that what at first seems one of the most important stumbling blocks in the path of faith in God, when examined more closely is seen to be part of a system based on perfect wisdom which, rather than obscuring the care of a father God, reveals and confirms it.

CHAPTER IV

WHY IS ATHEISM UNREASONABLE?

Now let us turn to convincing proofs indicating that the denial of God is quite unreasonable and showing that when we have these proofs in mind it is extremely difficult for a normal intelligent person to remain an atheist.

BEAUTY, TRUTH, AND GOODNESS

To any reasonable person who reflects deeply on the matter, it is evident that the presence in the world of the entities beauty, truth, and goodness all point to the existence of God. If, as we have seen, the presence of sin and pain presents problems for those who believe in God, the presence of the qualities of beauty, truth, and goodness present a much greater problem to those who would deny God. For if there is nothing higher and better than the material, then it is extremely difficult, if not quite impossible, to account for the existence of such qualities as beauty, truth, and goodness.

Why should beauty be found everywhere in the world? For what purpose is the infinite variety of beautiful colors? Why is it that in practically everything, from the tiniest plant, so small it can only be seen through a microscope, to the mighty sweep of the Himalaya mountains, loveliness and beauty are universal. There are some sorts of beauty of which it may be said there exists a material advantage. It can be said that physical beauty in living creatures has the effect of attracting mates and so perpetuating the species. Yet when we recall that even the least attractive individual usually does find a mate, and that the strength and endurance of the offspring are much more significant than the beauty of the mother in guaranteeing their survival, and that a beautiful frail wife may have no children, or at most one or two, while the unattractive but sturdy wife may have a dozen or more children, we see that beauty has a very limited value in perpetuating the species. And in this material world we find the universe to be filled with lovely sights which do not have the least importance in perpetuating life.

For example, if there is not a God, who is desirous of the happiness of his children, why should so common a thing as water appear in so many and varied beautiful states? Consider the small brooks with their calm fluid loveliness, the dashing streams sparkling in the sunlight, waterfalls with lovely rainbows in their spray, summer rains with the sunlight shining through the raindrops, all composed of nothing but water. Note the lovely rainbows after the summer rain—like a magic bridge across the heavens, reflect on the massive cloud formations sailing over the blue sky, then the golden tinge as sunset approaches, turning to pink, red, and finally purple and mauve. Observe the menacing black of the storm cloud spreading across the sky and heralding a summer deluge, and remember that these clouds are merely water. Notice the entirely new and different beauties to be seen when the weather turns cold, and water appears in new shapes and forms. What delight there is in watching the gentle snowflakes falling, and in studying their beautiful crystals, each different from every other, despite the fact that there are countless billions of them. How lovely the figures in the frost that gathers on the window pane during a night of intense cold, each different from every other and each a revelation of crystal beauty. Reflect on the varied beauties of ice formations, the smooth crystal clear ice on a calm unruffled lake, the massive glaciers slowly moving mountains of green and white ice, then the stately icebergs slowly melting as they sail to the south. Then there are the fascinating formations of icicles hanging from a thousand roofs, each a dagger pointed at the heart of the snow field below. There are the gentle aspects of water, such as the dew drops that may be seen clinging to the branches of the bushes and trees after a night of rain. As the morning sun strikes them, one is a liquid scarlet, another clear white as a diamond. Others are deep green like perfect emeralds, and still others a pale blue or delicate yellow. At the other extreme, stand on the seashore as the ocean waves, driven by a high wind, crash and break against the rocks on the shore, with a constant roar and mighty power that pounds the rocks into sand. The marvel is not so much that water should exist in all these forms, but that each and every form has a unique and perfect beauty of its own.

Now what is the purpose or practical use of all this beauty? It must be one of two things. Either these limitless beauties are the work of a good God who desires his children to be happy, or else their presence is a fathomless mystery without any reasonable cause. Look on the green pine forests whose dark calm rests and relaxes the spirit of one who enters them, and on the bewildering beauties of the desert after the winter rains, the beauty of the soft moss on the rocks, the alluring massive beauty of the stars at night. From the bottom of the coral reef which grows at the bottom of the sea, to the highest peak of Mt. Everest the world is crammed with beauty, universal and eternal. For those who believe in God the rays of the sun in the daytime and the silver beams of the moon shining mysteriously at night, are natural and understandable, indeed are necessary, but for others—who have other beliefs—it is an insoluble mystery.

For people who do not believe in God, the presence in this world of a passionate desire for the truth is an insoluble riddle. From where does this desire come? Whence comes the conviction that a man should speak the truth even when to do so is dangerous for him? Certainly in past ages before life had appeared on this earth such a respect and concern for truth was nowhere to be found. Lifeless water and earth most assuredly did not care about the truth, lifeless as they were and incapable of distinguishing truth from falsehood. This feeling of respect for truth did not even begin with the first appearance of life in the world. In the animal world there is no feeling of regret or repentance in regard to deception or treachery.

But when we come to man, we find here something new. Man tells lies. Most men—on occasion—will lie, and yet there is a sense of obligation and honor in man such that when he lies, he feels uneasy and ashamed. In his heart he knows that he has done something wrong. In the Gospel we read how the Apostle Peter one night, overcome with fear, denies even knowing Jesus Christ, and then we read how—some weeks later—this same Peter casts all fear aside and before the rulers of his people boldly testifies to his faith in Christ. I am sure none would deny that the Peter who bravely confessed his faith was a far finer man than the Peter who denied Him in order to avoid danger. Even the most dishonest Iranian today takes pride in the fact that his ancestors in the days of Darius and Cyrus were famous for speaking the truth. And there are few indeed in the world who do not consider being called a liar an insult.

This being the case, from whence does this feeling of reverence for the truth, even speaking the truth when it is dangerous to life to do so, come? In the natural world before the creation of man, there was no such idea. Can we imagine that a natural world which had no sense of right and wrong and could not see anything wrong in deceit and trickery, was able to produce a creature which possesses this power? Or is it more reasonable to believe that this sensitivity is the gift of the God of truth who Himself possesses such integrity? Certainly this faculty which is not possessed by other species must have been given to man for some special reason. The fact that this quality was not visible in the early stages of the development of the world cannot be taken as a proof that it was nowhere in existence, and then developed gradually. When a baby is first born, there is not the slightest indication of its special talents, social, musical or spiritual, and when these talents appear later no one considers them to be inventions of the baby, or the product of its environment. The truth is that this aptitude was always there and as time went on slowly made itself known. A stone never had such a quality but the child possessed it because his father had it before him, and he inherited the quality. It is more reasonable to believe that the Creation had this quality from the first as an inheritance from the father God, rather than that man developed this all by himself. It is far more logical to think that this sensibility to right and wrong is a gift from the One who possesses it in perfection and has passed it on to us.

Even more significant is the existence of unselfishness and self denial and self sacrifice in the human race. Scientists teach that self preservation is the first law of nature, and in general this is true. But in man, and in some of the higher animals, another law, self sacrifice for the good of others, appears. A ship at sea begins to go down. There are hundreds of men, women and children aboard. There are not enough life boats to save all the passengers. The cry goes up: "Women and children first." The men draw back so that the women and children can get aboard the life boats while the men go down with the ship. Why? The men have plenty of strength to hold back the others and save themselves, but they do not do this. An English doctor named Dr. Ross hears of the spread of a deadly disease known as sleeping sickness in central Africa. This disease has a fatality rate of one hundred percent. One who contracts it never recovers. He himself has a prosperous practice in England. Yet he leaves his home, goes to equatorial Africa in order to combat this disease and, if possible, to save the lives of thousands of savage, ignorant, and superstitious black men. Why? This conduct is entirely opposed to the law of self preservation, yet despite this the whole world voices its approval and appreciation.

From this we see that the higher one rises on the scale of life, to this same degree he becomes possessed with love, goodness and sacrifice. If the world is nothing but the material we cannot imagine where such qualities come from. Mud, rock and sand simply do not possess these qualities. And if there is no God, and no creator, then men must have been made by mud and water. We cannot possibly explain how, from lifeless elements, such high and spiritual qualities should develop. But if man is the creation of God, and is nearer to God than all other parts of creation, then it is not only possible but inevitable that he, more than other animals, should possess these special Godlike qualities. The more we rise in the scale of life, the closer we come to God. What is an insoluble mystery for the atheist is for the believer in God an inevitable crowning development. Goodness, reverence for truth, and beauty, all of these bring us assurance that there is a God.

For Every Need there is a Corresponding Provision

The unreasonableness of atheism becomes more evident when we recall that over against every felt need of living creatures there is something that meets that need, in the outside world. Before a child is born he is fully equipped for exercising the five senses, although at that time they are not of the slightest value to him. But as soon as he enters this world he finds himself in an environment where he could not survive without them. As we noted above, his eyes are fully developed when he is in total darkness where the eyes are completely useless. But later, when he enters a new world of light, his eyes become indispensable. The various organs for breathing, similarly, are completely developed in an environment where he cannot breathe, then suddenly he finds himself in a world surrounded by air, perfectly adapted to his lungs' needs. Likewise the organs of taste and smell, with all their intricate mechanism, are perfected in an environment where they are completely useless, and then suddenly become essential to life in his new environment. An elaborate digestive system is provided using the mouth, the teeth, the saliva glands, the throat, the stomach and the intestines, each with its own intricate interrelations with the other, all at a time when he cannot eat and has no use for them. Then suddenly he is in a new environment where the possession of just these faculties is a matter of life or death.

His life, after his birth, also reveals the same sort of provisions for all his needs. In the world about us there are plenty of materials for meeting each one of our needs, and satisfying each of our inner desires. Plenty of material provisions have been made to satisfy all of man's needs even though at times, because of his own ignorance or the opposition of others, he is not able to make use of them. Man needs clothing to protect his body from heat and cold and rain, and he finds himself in a world fully equipped with cotton, wool, linen, silk, skins and thousands of other materials with which to protect himself. He needs a dwelling place and the world offers him hundreds of varieties of wood, stone, metals and the materials for making bricks, blocks of ice in the north, and long grasses in hot climates. With the changing seasons he needs facilities for traveling from one place to another, and the world is ready with the horse, the donkey, the camel, the cow, the dog, the llama and the reindeer, and in addition numberless materials from which he can make the railway, the automobile and the airplane. He is attacked by diseases and discovers he is in a world where countless seeds, roots and grasses are found with medicinal value, and he finds that from other available materials he can concoct new drugs which are still more effective. Even though at the present time there are still diseases for which we have found no cure, still man presses steadily on in his investigations with the hope, and even the certainty, that eventually he will find the way to cure presently incurable diseases.

In the same way all sorts of provisions are found in this world for meeting the mental and spiritual needs of humankind. Man has a sense of beauty, and loves beautiful things, and—as we saw above—finds himself in a world that is crammed with beauty on every hand, to satisfy his inner hunger. His soul loves and longs for music, and he not only finds himself able to sing, and enjoy the singing of others, but also finds an abundance of materials from which he can construct the flute, the guitar, the horn or the piano, and indeed hundreds of other varieties of musical instruments. When one travels around the world and finds everywhere the countless varieties of musical instruments men have made, he is amazed at the abundance of provision this world contains. Man is created with curiosity and a desire to understand, and the world opens up before him a limitless store of secrets to be solved and mysteries to be unravelled, and it offers him strips of papyrus, materials for making paper, mud tablets and stone surfaces on which to record what he has found out.

He needs friendship and companionship and finds he is living in a world where there are endless opportunities for social contacts, the selection of a mate, the followship of an endless variety of organizations. Men everywhere sense their need for God. Wherever one goes he finds shrines and temples, churches and mosques, holy books and dedicated people searching for a knowledge of God. Is it conceivable that there should be provision for all the many types of need we have listed, but there is no provision for this deepest need of all. Can we imagine that alone among the felt needs of mankind, all of which have a corresponding reality to meet them, this one universal imperative corresponds with no reality and there is no one there? This is impossible to believe!

Perhaps some here would raise the question as to whether there really is a general deeply felt need for God, or a desire to worship Him. If so, the answer is written large on the pages of history. When we turn back to the earliest ages of the life of man we find that men did worship God or many gods. Go to whatever portion of the world you wish today and you will find this to be true. Some years ago archaeologists in southern France investigated some large caves in which men had lived some twenty thousand years ago. They had left on the walls of the cave colored pictures depicting their life at that early time. There they found clear and certain evidence that these ancient cave men were worshipping a power above and beyond themselves. In recent years scores of tombs have been opened up in Kurdistan and Luristan in Iran. In every one of them various implements were found, such as tools, beads, bronze daggers and battle axes, all of which were left there in the hope of their being useful on resurrection day. With these often a small idol is found also showing them to have been religious men and women. At this present time, go where you will in all the world and you will find those living there worshipping higher powers deemed useful for their style of life.

The land of Japan is full of places of worship, many of them strikingly beautiful, all of them erected for the worship of some god or gods. The outstandingly beautiful buildings of China, Thailand, India, and Pakistan are those which have been erected for the worship of their gods. In Jerusalem the famous Dome of the Rock, in Istanbul the Aya Sophia mosque, in Athens the Parthenon, in Rome St. Peter's, in Paris Notre Dame and in London St. Paul's—all are places of worship. Wherever one goes in the world the loveliest and most costly structures are the places of religious worship. All this is strong proof for the claim that man feels deeply the need for God.

In the same way the most beautiful books to be found in the world are the religious books. Other books come and go, are talked about and soon forgotten, but the religious books seem to be eternal. Whether in India or America, whether China or Iran, the most honored and loved books are the religious books. It is now nearly 2000 years since the death of Jesus, and yet the book that relates the story of his life is more widely circulated than any other book in the world. Whenever a modern novel which men admire reaches a total sale of one hundred thousand copies, this is considered remarkable. If after many years its total sales should reach a million, it is considered marvelous. Yet the New Testament, with its story of Jesus, sells in any given year not one hundred thousand, and not merely a million, but in whole or in part, sells over thirty million copies a year. There is no other book to compare with it. And men purchase it for this reason: that it tells them about God and how He is to be served and worshipped.

Therefore there is no doubt that the desire to serve God and the sense of need for God is not merely a universal human quality but probably the deepest of all feelings. In this case then, must we think that there is nothing in the universe to satisfy this longing and meet its need? Is it possible to believe that this world is so arranged as to meet the smallest physical need of man, and all of his social needs, but there is nothing to satisfy the deepest and most urgent spiritual need? Can we believe that corresponding to every intellectual and spiritual need, such as the love and longing for beauty, the need for music and melody, the need for love and fellowship, there is something in the universe that corresponds with the need and makes it possible to satisfy it, but in response to the most fundamental and deepest need there is nothing there? Surely this is impossible to accept. Just as the physical needs of man demand that there should be something in the world to meet those needs, just as all other mental and spiritual needs of men are found to have a corresponding provision to meet them, just so we can feel certain that this deep universal need of mankind for a heavenly father, a Creator he wishes to know and worship is not a vain and senseless hunger with nothing to satisfy it. It is not merely possible but essential that there should be some such reality. In other words, let us say that just as the eye is an organ for discerning light, and the ear is for hearing outside sound, and the sense of taste is for enjoying food, and longing for a mate corresponds with her existence, and the love for beauty is met with a beauty-filled world, and the love for harmony is satisfied with the songs of the birds, man's own ability to produce music, and his God-given skill in making musical instruments, just so must the sense of need for God have been given to man in response to one outside himself who can meet his need. And that outside one is what we call God. It is impossible to believe that there should be this quality in all the world that every need presupposes something to meet it, and that something is always to be found that does meet it, or to believe that for every thirst in man there is something to quench it, with one exception, and that exception should be in regard to the deepest of all human needs: the need of the soul for God.

THE RESULTS OF ATHEISM

In addition to the above considerations, atheism and the denial of God is seen to be unreasonable from another angle, and that is the effect that such a belief has on man's conduct. It is true, of course, that there are many whose characters have been formed in an atmosphere of faith in God, and who later have lost their faith, and who—without realizing it—are living by the standards of religion which they learned long ago. In their lives it is obvious that their characters and points of view are not the product of atheism. But when this atheistic philosophy has been fully accepted and has become the foundation of one's life and conduct, its inevitable results undermine the bases of civilization and character and endeavor.

The first result of accepting atheism is a feeling of weakness, despair and hopelessness. For the atheist knows that however much we strive and struggle, and however many brilliant successes we achieve, in the end it all comes to nothing and is quite useless. If there is no God, then man's condition is like the position of a polar bear drifting toward warm water on an iceberg, with the certainty that the ice beneath him will all turn to water and he will perish. There is no doubt that this world is headed for oblivion. If it does not disappear as a result of the explosion of the sun or some similar catastrophe, the world will itself grow colder and colder until it is no longer capable of supporting any form of life. By then all memory of a human race shall have passed away. This being the case, what good result can come from all of our strivings, and what useful purpose will it all have served? All of our castles and buildings, all of our dams and bridges, all the human wisdom stored up in countless books and magazines, will have no readers and these books themselves will moulder to dust, and all of our struggles and efforts for improvement and progress will be useless and forgotten.

Under these conditions what is the use of struggle and work and striving? Why struggle for the advancement of science and learning, why labor in the cause of salvation, spiritual progress and honor? It is certain that in time we shall be driven back and defeated. If we are highly successful in our endeavors at best we can only add a few years to this trouble-filled existence, but in the end it will end in nothingness. Everyone who has a mind and learning and actually believes that this world is nothing more than what we see, must logically adopt for himself a life philosophy based on a paralyzing belief in hopelessness and despair. Life with enterprise and activity is like a mirage in the desert and the nerves of decision and action will be severed. It is of course true that at a time of some great national crisis, such as invasion by foreign armies, or under the drive of some five year plan, man may for the time being forget all this in striving to meet the present goal or danger, and act as though it were possible to achieve lasting success in this world. But when he believes the opposite, he will not for any length of time be willing to engage in such useless struggle. Certainly a general belief in the vanity of all effort will not suffice to undergird a whole civilization.

In addition, if the materialists and atheists are right, man is not a spiritual being, and all of his feelings and thoughts are the result of chemical reactions in the brain. If this is the case, of what special value is a man, and why should we think an individual has any rights, rights that others should honor? If we should be upset because others do not give the proper honor and respect to a bottle of chemicals, we would reveal our own folly. For if we take the soul of a man, all that remains is a bottle of chemicals. In this case spilling the blood of a human being is no worse than pouring out a glassful of mineral water on the ground, and an individual man entirely loses his worth. This being the case we are not exaggerating if we maintain that the foundation of civilization rests on the value attached to each individual. The difference between humans and civilized governments and savagery is just this. In truly civilized countries, every single individual, rich or poor, young or old, wise or untrained, possesses inalienable rights and his value beyond all reckoning. But in savage or backward lands it is not so. In civilized lands orphan children are cared for with moving concern in orphanages, or given to responsible foster parents to bring up, but in savage tribes they are left to shift for themselves and to beg for a living or starve to death. In civilized lands old people, if they are indigent, are cared for in special homes, or given allowances by their governments to keep them alive and well. But in the South Seas, for example, before the coming of the Christian faith, older people were killed off as a nuisance and perhaps eaten. In savage places women are considered like animals, but little superior to a horse or dog. But in civilized countries they are protected and honored. Infanticide, warfare and murder are part of the normal life of savage tribes. But in civilized lands they deplore and oppose warfare and constantly strive to rid the world of this scourge.

Possibly the greatest service Christianity has made to civilization is that it has revealed and emphasized the value of every individual. The teaching that God loves even the worst of sinners and wishes that he find salvation; that Christ came to this world to die not for the good and pious men and women, but to save sinners crushed by the weight of their sins, the teaching that the spirit may possess eternal life, all these teachings reveal the worth of the individual.

Jesus asked: "What shall it profit a man if he gain the whole world and lose his own soul?" (Matthew 16:26; Mark 8:36; Luke 9:25). From this question we can see that the spirit of a man is the most precious thing in all the world of material and physical elements. It is on this account that whenever the teachings of Christ have gone to places where terror and oppression ruled supreme, they have brought a new style of life.

Later on in this writing we shall treat this matter more fully. At this point it is enough to point out that the most important and significant single belief for achieving and maintaining the rights of man, and, as a result, for the progress and spread of true civilization, is this conviction that the individual human being possesses worth and value beyond exaggeration. Nor is there any logic in saying that the individual has no value, but society has infinite value—for the sum of a thousand zeroes is still a zero. And if each human being is without value, we cannot believe that a million of them are valuable. It is on this account that the principles of materialism destroy the foundations of civilized life. For just as the loss of a sense of the value of the individual everywhere and always results in cruelty and savagery—so the loss of faith in God which is the foundation of man's belief in individual worth is bound to deal a deadly blow to civilization. Is it possible or reasonable or logical that truth should be something that finally makes the growth of civilization impossible? Is it possible to believe that the acceptance of mistaken ideas should bring the finest results while the truth would produce decay and destruction? In a world of cause and effect, such as is our world, such a conclusion is totally contrary to logic and reason. Truth is something which results in improvement and happiness. Falsehood is something that would undermine and destroy that growth and improvement. Thus it is evident that materialistic atheism, being totally opposed to what leads to progress and growth, must be a false theory. On the other hand, belief in God, which is the source of beneficial results, must be essentially true.

CHAPTER V

PROOFS FROM EXPERIENCES OF THE REALITY OF GOD

Up to this point all of our proofs have been intellectual, based on reasoning and logic, but there is another series of proofs which are more important and convincing than these, and they are the proofs that come from experience. By and large what we really know are the things we have been able to experience personally. We accept much on the basis of the statements of others, but what we actually know are those facts which are part of our personal experience. In religion also, this is true. The ultimate proof for the existence of God must be based on actual experience. If this belief works out in practice then not only will it persist, but it is evidently true. But if it fails to meet the test of life, then sooner or later it will pass away, however reasonable it might seem to be.

EXPERIENCE OF THE EXPERTS

Let us first of all look at the experience of the specialists in this field. What have they learned about religious truth? Our age is one in which in every branch of learning we have to depend on the words of the experts. When Iran determined to avail itself of the developments of western civilization, its first step was to invite advisors; legal advisors, customs, police, roads, finance, tea culture, education, railway. It invited men who are specialists in these various fields and moved forward in accordance with their recommendations, even when the reason for some of them was not clear. Then when it saw that the results of accepting their advice were beneficial, it was glad to continue to follow their guidance. Indeed the advance of learning in the twentieth century is so swift and varied that no one man can hope to comprehend more than a tiny portion of the whole, and even what the expert knows comes to him largely on the basis of the witness of other experts.

Every educated man has studied geography. Yet how much of his knowledge of geography has he gained at first hand? If he has traveled a great deal he may have seen a few towns and cities near his birthplace and possibly the important ports of several other countries. Even so, he will not have seen a thousandth part of the islands, rivers, lakes and seas that are carefully drawn in the maps he has studied. And in regard to those places he has not seen personally, if he wishes to learn all possible facts regarding them he must depend on the word of the experts. Even so he does not consider himself ignorant of geography and speaks with confidence of the geographical facts of places he has never seen, relying on the witness of the specialists and travelers. In the realm of astronomy, how many of us who delight in the marvels revealed in the heavens have personally made astronomical investigations? We have been told that the sun is ninety-three million miles from the earth, that it is a million times as large as the earth, and that its temperature on the surface is 6000 degrees Centigrade. We accept these statements without hesitation. But how many of us have ever measured the distance to the sun, or observed a thermometer which measures its heat? We accept the word of astronomers whom we have never met and whose names, in all probability, we do not know, because they are experts in this field and we are confident that they are speaking the truth. When we fall sick we at once send for a doctor. Perhaps we have never seen him before and have never heard of the medicine he gives us. All the same, we take the prescribed medicine because he is a specialist in medicine and we are not. Thus it is not in the least unreasonable if in the matter of religion also we inquire of the experts, to see what they can tell us.

It may be that before we take the expert's word we should like to ask two questions. One is this: "Is the man to whom I am turning actually an expert in this field?" The other is: "Is this man reliable?" In this regard we must bear in mind that a man may be highly trained as a specialist in one field, but be quite uninformed in regard to matters outside his field. For instance, when we wish to learn of the most recent developments in the realm of physics, we inquire of a physicist, and not of a politician. On the other hand, when we wish information on political developments, we turn to the politician—not to the professor of physics.

Perhaps at first sight this seems too obvious to be worth pointing out, but actually it is very important, because today there are many who think that the views of a chemist, for example, in regard to religion, are highly significant because he is a well-known scientist, whereas it has no special importance unless he may also have made a special study of religion, and in this field also can speak with authority. They say that one time the famous philosopher and scientist, Isaac Newton, sent for a carpenter and asked him to make two small openings in the door to his study. He explained that often when he was engrossed in some difficult problem, his cat would come to the door and mew until he came to open the door, thus distracting him from his work. When the carpenter asked why he wanted two little doors he replied that the cat had a small kitten, and the little door was for its use. Not until the carpenter pointed it out had it occurred to him that the small kitten could go out by the larger door prepared for its mother. When Isaac Newton spoke in regard to some mathematical process, the whole world listened to what he had to say, as he was the first mathematician of his age. But when the matter involved was a door for a cat and her kittens, a village carpenter could give him guidance.

Very few people in the world's history have opened more new doors to science than the famous Charles Darwin. It has been pointed out that at least six modern branches of science have developed from his studies and writings, and few indeed are the thinkers whose ideas have been more fruitful. Despite this, Charles Darwin, toward the end of his life, observed that the intense love of music which he had enjoyed during his younger days had been so neglected and unused that he could no longer find any enjoyment in music and could, with difficulty, distinguish one tune from another. This man was one of the great pioneer thinkers whose books will be read for many years to come, yet he was so backward in music that a high school student could have given him lessons.

On this account, at the same time we recognize that the world is indebted to the scholars in physics, chemistry, astronomy and the like who, by their tireless investigations, have brought about revolutions in man's understanding and has a right to give the highest importance to what they have to say in the realms of their specialties, it is a great mistake to consider them as automatically authorities in the realm of religion. When we are searching for religious truth what is important to us is the testimony of religious experts. Therefore the first question we must ask is: Is this person a specialist in this branch of knowledge?

The second question is this: "Is this witness reliable?" If he is dependable then we accept without reservations what he says he has personally seen and heard. Specialists in religion are those who have spent their lives in searching out and performing God's will, and tell us of their experiences. The Bible, for example, is a book of witness. This book is largely composed of the biographies of individuals who have spent their lifetime in understanding the truth about God and his will for men, and are reporting their experiences. At this point there is no disagreement between atheists and believers because both accept the fact that these individuals are specialists in religion. So only the second question remains, namely are these men reliable witnesses? There can be no doubt that not all those who claimed to be prophets spoke the truth. There are many of them who contradict each other. But this difficulty can be overcome. It seems obvious that those who have sought material advantage from their teaching and have used it to become wealthy and famous are people whose testimony is lacking in importance or value. Similarly, those who have taught that lying and dissimulation are all right cannot expect to be believed. But when we read the histories of the prophets, as written in the Holy Bible, we realize that without exaggeration, they are to be classed as the most truthful and truth loving people of all time. They were people to whom a lie was abhorrent. In order that the truth might be evident they endangered their lives in order to lead others to the truth, whereas they could have had safe and quiet lives had they only kept silent. It is utterly impossible to suppose that such men were liars. These are men who are certain they have learned the truth about God and are constantly risking their lives in order to give the good news to others. They repeatedly and confidently proclaim: "Thus saith the Lord." We cannot easily reject their testimony. Whatever be the matter under consideration, it is usually considered true when two or three men of integrity testify to its truth. How much more then the reality of God's existence is affirmed, not by two or three but by scores of the most reliable and discerning men whom the world has ever seen, who have written down their experiences for our guidance.

Of course it may be argued that these are reliable men but they were deceived or mistaken. The extreme improbability that this was the case becomes evident when we look at their extraordinary spiritual qualities and the deep impression their lives have made. It is impossible to believe that their unselfishness and amazing humility, their outstanding courage, the influence of their personalities, and their vision and discernment should all spring from a mistaken philosophy and lives built upon a delusion.

THE INFLUENCE OF THE LIFE OF ONE WHOLLY DEVOTED TO GOD

Another evidence for the reality of God based upon experience is the amazing influence of a life entirely based upon a belief in God and the conviction that man's first duty is obedience to God's commands. If there is no God, and this theory is entirely mistaken, then we should expect that a life based on the mistaken theory should be fruitless and useless. But if there is a God, then the life of one who most of all was obedient to his commands should deeply affect the life of the world. What makes the influence of Jesus Christ impressive is not merely that he was a believer and a prophet as others had been, but that he completely rejected material aids for his work and depended entirely upon God.

For example, Jesus could have amassed large sums of money in return for his healing ministry and, by using this money, he could have spread his teachings to all parts of the world. There are those who have done this. For example, Mary Baker Eddy founded a new religion in America some years ago. By charging very high fees for her lessons she was able to raise hundreds of thousands of dollars, and thereby to print millions of pamphlets regarding her teaching, send them to all parts of the world, and also to erect large and beautiful places of worship. She was not the only one to do this sort of thing. Others have laid down the law that when their followers were guilty of some sin, they should pay a heavy fine to the leader and founder. Others have organized armies and fought until portions of the globe fell under their power. Some of these gained considerable power during their lifetimes, but it is always possible to argue that their success and influence were not because they taught the truth, but because of the backing of their wealth. Obviously, as noted above, it would have been very easy for Jesus to have acquired wealth. Such a wonderful healer could have gathered large amounts of money for the advancement of his cause. Wealthy people were attracted by his teaching, yet when one wealthy young man wished to become his disciple, Jesus instructed him first to go, sell all his goods and give to the poor and then come and follow him. He resolutely refused all the financial aid he could have received from this wealthy man, and persisted in this course to the end of his life, so that he was utterly poor, lacking any possessions. As he himself pointed out, the birds and the foxes had their homes but he had no place of his own to lay his head. When they killed him he owned nothing but the clothes he wore that his murderers might seize, and when he died they buried him in another's grave. Thus no one can account for his impact and influence by attributing it to his money.

Another means whereby men are won over, and whereby followers are won is the assistance of powerful friends. Some have striven by every means to secure powerful and influential friends. They have written letters and approached kings, presidents, statesmen and leaders in their search for big and influential followers. But Jesus took an entirely different course. He spent his lifetime in the company of ordinary men and women. When King Herod tried to talk with him he gave no reply. He sought out his followers from the poorest and least esteemed classes. One of his twelve chosen disciples was a Zealot, or revolutionary, who had been plotting to overthrow the Roman government. Another was a tax collector, a member of the most despised profession in Palestine, whom his fellow Jews considered to be a traitor to his country and almost certainly a thief as well. A number of his followers were fishermen. It would have been hard to find a group of men whose words would have less influence on the educated classes, the philosophers and the heads of religion. There was not a single wealthy man, and most of them were poorly educated. There was not a priest or lawyer or government official among them. So, whatever the cause of Jesus' influence, it certainly did not come from the fact that he had powerful friends—for he had none.

Another way to success and successful leadership is for someone to seize political power, make himself dictator or emperor, for instance, and thus lay down and enforce laws and regulations which please him.

The political life of most nations is largely determined by the ambitions of men who wish to rise to positions of power and influence. Some of these are true patriots who wish to introduce better laws and customs in place of ancient and inadequate ones. Others are purely selfish individuals whose motives are personal glory and enrichment. But the tactics of both are very similar. In order to realize their inner desire they must obtain a position of leadership and control so that they may realize their goals. This path was open to Jesus, who could have followed it had he wished. One of his earliest temptations came when it was proposed to him that if he should follow Satan's leadership he could have the rulership of all the world. He rejected this temptation vigorously. Later on when he fed over five thousand persons in the wilderness from five barley loaves and two small fish, the crowd wished to make him their king on the spot. They were sure that should he speak the word all of Galilee would rise to his support. But when he saw what they were planning, he immediately left them and spent the night in prayer to God. Thus he rejected this policy. He was determined to rely solely on God and on spiritual means to advance his cause.

A fourth path which he might easily have trod was that of making war, a path which a great many leaders and reformers beyond counting have felt themselves obliged to follow. The Jewish people expected that their Messiah should do this. One of their happiest dreams was of the time when Christ should come and drive the Romans from their land. Jesus' followers also cherished this expectation, and were prepared to fight. Their hatred of the Romans was so intense and their desire for freedom from slavery to Rome was so deep, that had Jesus unsheathed the sword and called on them to follow him, hundreds of thousands would have at once responded, and gathered around him. How easy it would have been to set up the Kingdom by war and violence, wipe out all of his enemies and turn the Kingdom over to those who would support him. But Jesus refused to follow this course also. When Peter drew the sword in order to defend him, Jesus ordered him: "Put up thy sword in its sheath, for they that draw the sword will perish by the sword" (Matthew 26:52; John 18:11). In this way Jesus once again reveals his complete trust in his heavenly Father.

In this way we see for the first time in the history of the world a unique man who wished to accomplish a complete revolution in the world and establish a new path of life and character and thinking, and yet did not use any of the material means which all others have felt necessary and inevitable. If the world is fundamentally material, and if there is nothing but material objects in the world, and God and spirit are nothing but baseless superstitions, then beyond doubt such a life would not have the slightest effect on this world. It would be like trying to build a skyscraper on air. All efforts and striving would end in failure. While, on the contrary, if Jesus spoke the truth, and if there is a God, and if the spiritual is not merely real but is the only eternal reality, then a life that is lived in harmony with God and for the perfection of the spirit, will be more influential than every other sort of life. Which of these two possibilities is revealed by Jesus' life? Everyone knows the answer to this question. We find no one else in all history today who, two thousand years after his death, has as many followers as has Christ. Here the verdict of William E. H. Lecky, the rationalist historian, is unqualified as he says: "The simple record of three short years of [Christ's] active life has done more to regenerate and to soften mankind than all the disquisitions of philosophers, and all the exhortations of moralists" (*History of European Morals from Augustus to Charlemagne*, II, 9 [New York, 1884]).

From this we arrive at this result, and in reaching it, it makes no difference whether we are Muslim or Christian, Jew or atheist, that the influence of Jesus Christ on the world is a living proof that his life was founded on a sound theory. If we see that an engineer erects a dam that cannot stand up under the test of time, but after a few years collapses and is swept away, while another engineer builds a dam that lasts a thousand years, we would inevitably conclude that the second engineer was the one who knew the principles of engineering, not the first. Just so is it with human life. When we see that the influence of all those who lived in the first century, and built their lives on the principles of wealth, worldly power, political maneuvering and the sword, did not last beyond their own days, and men today by and large do not even know their names, while the influence of Him who built his life on a faith in God is infinitely greater and still increases day by day, we have the right to conclude that the life of this man was founded on the truth, and not the others.

Review of the Effects of Jesus' Teaching About God

When one compares the condition of the countries where men best obey the teachings of Jesus with lands where his teaching is unknown, or with the condition of those lands before they heard his teaching, then he can discern how the life and influence of Christ has brought countless benefits and blessings. If his teachings were false or fundamentally mistaken, there is no way of explaining where these blessings and benefits came from. But if, on the contrary, his teachings are founded on the truth then such benefits and blessings are the natural result of his teachings.

Of course no one claims that the countries that are called Christian countries have become perfect. There is no place in the world where even half of the population are striving with all their might to obey all his teachings. But in every country in the world where the teachings of Christ have become well known, and the people have accepted them in sincerity, amazing progress has resulted, while in every area of life where his teachings have not been followed—even though they call themselves Christians—glaring defects remain. This is all that one can ask. Our basis for judgment is not what are the results of Jesus' life where his teachings are not obeyed, but rather what is the effect when they are put to work? If we wish to know how effective a physician is, we do not ask of those who never turned to him for help, and never had him prescribe for their illnesses, but rather we test his skill by inquiring of those who have obeyed his instructions what the results have been.

First of all, the progress in science and learning in countries that have obeyed Christ's teachings, attract our attention; here, without exaggeration, we may say that the influence of no one in the history of the world has compared with the effect of Jesus' teaching in this regard. From the time when he instructed his apostles to go out and teach all nations his teachings have been a steadily increasing light to lighten all nations. The early Christians felt obliged to teach their children how to read and write and to train them according to Jesus' teachings. During the centuries known as the Dark Ages, when savage tribes from central Europe overwhelmed European civilization and threatened to completely destroy it, Christian monasteries were as a light in the darkness, where they preserved and developed ancient learning. Christian missionaries went out among these savage tribes and opened schools for them. The Bible has been translated in whole or in part into over 1200 languages today, and in most of these languages the first book to be translated was the Bible, and the missionaries were the ones who devised an alphabet and opened their first schools. This means that in over 900 peoples and tongues the foundations of learning were laid by Christian missionaries, who entered their lands when they had no written languages and no schools and opened up to them the outside world of science and learning.

This progress continues to the present time. Some years ago reports showed over 41,000 schools operating under mission auspices in foreign lands, in which over 2 million students were studying. Many countries in the past have opened schools to train their own children. It is only the Christian churches which have opened these thousands of schools in foreign and distant lands, and usually they were opened at the risk of the lives who went to strange and often hostile lands for this service. Thus the teachings of Jesus, quite aside from their moral and religious effect, have done more than any other power to widen the outreach of learning and science. So once again we are faced with the necessity of deciding between two explanations. Either there is a God, so Jesus' teaching was founded on the truth, or there is no God and all of these beneficial and sacrificial services are based on empty superstition. When we consider the results of this teaching in promoting the progress of the human race, which of the two explanations seems logical and reasonable?

A second result of the spread of Jesus' teachings in regard to God is the development of a new sensitivity to the needs of the poor and a feeling of responsibility for their welfare. Before the spread of his teaching in most lands there was no provision for the care of orphans, but orphans were left to wander in the streets where most of them died from hunger and exposure.

Similarly, those who could not find work, or were physically disabled so they could not work, had no recourse but to become beggars by the way. In Rome, in order to keep the populace quiet, wheat was distributed freely from time to time, and of course there were kind people who would give them alms and try to help them. But the Christian teaching that God loves the poorest and most unfortunate individuals awakened people to the fact that their responsibility was not met by doling out a few cents to a beggar, but demanded that some permanent provision be made for his care. The early Christians were mostly from the poorer classes, yet from the very beginning they would set aside certain days for fasting, so that they could give the money saved to the poor. In the following centuries Christian leaders provided permanent homes and care for such unfortunates. St. Basil was the first to erect a home for lepers which he opened on the bank of the Euphrates River in the fourth century, where he also opened a public hospital. St. Pammuchus, about the same time, also founded a public hospital. Thalasius opened a home for blind beggars on the banks of the Euphrates. The Council of Nice directed that refuges for strangers and travelers be erected in every city. Thus, gradually throughout the Christian world provisions were made for the poor, the crippled, the sick and the unfortunate. During the Dark Ages the Christian monasteries were not merely schools as we noted above, but also were hospitals for the sick, refuges for the oppressed and homes for the destitute. For the first time in the history of the human race thousands of men and women were moved by Christian teachings to dedicate their entire lives to relieving the troubles of the unfortunate, despite the pains, troubles and sacrifices they incurred.

These sorts of services to humanity continue down to the present. Wherever the teachings of Christ have gone, the foundations have been laid for countless varieties of services to those in need. Homes have been provided for the poor, the orphans, the aged, the insane, the lepers, the crippled and the blind. Each new war or disaster anywhere in the world is met with aid from Christian foundations. Church World Service, an arm of the World Council of Christian churches, in the year 1964 aided over six million persons in 40 countries and shipped nearly two hundred thousand tons of clothing to war refugees and disaster victims. And this is but one of many Christian organizations working to relieve human suffering.

It must be remembered that before the tribes of western Europe and America had accepted the teachings of Christ such a spirit was not dreamed of. Rather each tribe felt a sense of relief if members of another tribe suffered hunger and want, as that meant they would be weaker and more easily conquered. But after they had accepted the faith in one God revealed in Christ, they were impelled to give enormous sums of money for aiding their neighbors, and even for aiding the most distant countries. Can we then think that the faith in a loving God which so transformed those savage tribes, is a baseless superstition? Can all of these fruits be gathered from a dead and lifeless tree?

Another change in men's conduct toward one another resulting from their accepting Christ's teaching about God, relates to the fate of slaves. When Jesus came, the common practice was to take all prisoners of war who had not been killed at the time of victory and sell them into slavery. As a result, the cities of the Roman Empire were crowded with slaves, there being twice as many slaves as free men. Although many of these were well treated, so far as the law was concerned they had no rights. Their owners might command them to fight against each other to the death in order to amuse their owners. If a slave owner should be murdered, all of his slaves were executed for not protecting him. Slaves were not allowed to marry and when they cohabited and children were born, the children were the property of the owner, and were sold to others. A slave might be killed for the slightest error or offense. History tells of one slave owner who ordered a slave cut to pieces so he could find out whether the carp in his pool would eat human flesh.

But the belief in one God, the Father of all, and that men therefore are brothers of one another, brought with it a different viewpoint on these unfortunates. It became the custom for the churches to take up special offerings for freeing the slaves, and huge sums were raised for this purpose, and it became the custom to purchase the release of slaves and to set them free in the Church on Easter morning. One church succeeded in freeing 1,400 slaves, another 5,000 slaves and another church 8,000 slaves. By the beginning of the Middle Ages, slavery had practically disappeared, but as a result of the upheavals and wars of that period, many were obliged to sell themselves into slavery and the custom of slavery revived. Once again the churches began to collect money to buy the freedom of these slaves until by the fourteenth century there was no longer any slavery in Europe, and instead of setting slaves free on Easter Day the churches had to set free pigeons. Later, as a result of the opening up of Africa and the demand for cheap labor in the newly discovered lands of America, slavery reappeared and flourished in the colonies. This time Christian pioneers such as Wilberforce in England and Garrison in America mobilized the opposition of Christians and the practice was outlawed. Today this evil custom only prevails in a few out-of-the-way places such as central Arabia and equatorial Africa, and the influence of Christian nations through the United Nations is steadily diminishing the extent of this practice. In this way, and as a result of Jesus' teaching, the accursed yoke of slavery which millions of unfortunates had borne through all ages of the history of mankind, was broken and cast away. Once again we ask the question, was the basis for this amazing victory for mankind an error, an empty illusion, or is it reasonable to conclude that it came from a spread of the truth?

Another river of blessing which has flowed from the teachings and example of Christ is a new concern for the care and cure of the sick. For us who think of adequate hospitals and medical care as one of the necessary pillars of civilization, it is a cause for astonishment to learn that the ancient civilizations of Greece and Iran and Rome had no public hospitals. It was only in the fourth century A.D. that a Christian woman named Fabiola opened the first public hospital in the world's history. And not only in the hospitals, but also in the care of the sick at home the monks and nuns introduced new and better methods. When an epidemic of the plague devastated Carthage in 326 A.D., tens of thousands of the idolators fled the city, but the monks and nuns stood their ground and large numbers came from other places to help. Many of them lost their lives in this service, but they first had shown the world something new and different, that is a love such as to compel men and women to sacrifice their lives for others, even those who were their enemies.

It is utterly impossible to compute the amount of aid and assistance which Christian doctors and nurses have rendered to the sick in all parts of the world to non-Christian peoples. In 1958 it was reported that such hospitals had a total of 65,989 beds and were caring for

1,580,988 inpatients a year and nearly nine million outpatients. In these hospitals 1,379 national doctors and 883 missionary doctors were serving, aided by 6,057 national nurses and 1,411 missionary nurses. One of the most beneficial results of the founding of these hospitals has been their awakening local governments to their need for hospitals, with the result that in practically every land where the first hospitals were founded by foreign Christian missionaries, the local governments have followed their examples and opened similar government-run hospitals, and also opened medical schools to train their young people in western medicine. Public health departments, schools for training nurses, hospital aids, and midwives, the establishment of quarantines, homes for lepers, institutions which every day serve millions of people—all owe their origin to that first public hospital founded by men and women who believed God was their Father, a God of love who commanded them to serve one another. And it is that same belief that today undergirds hospitals all over the world. Again we ask, is the belief that produces such massive help and healing a baseless superstition? Is it only a childish mistake to be overcome? To say so is like saying that strychnine is food and bread is poison. It makes nonsense of the laws of cause and effect and contravenes reason and logic.

INDIVIDUAL EXPERIENCE

The most complete and convincing proof of the reality of God so far as the individual is concerned is his personal experience of God's reality. Like many other branches of learning, the final proof comes from putting the theory to the test. Whether theoretical proofs are decisive or not, no sane man can deny his own experience. The blind man whom Jesus had cured, in the face of all objections and criticisms, could only say: "One thing I know, that whereas I was blind, now I see" (John 9:25). In the same way our most certain and unshakable convictions and the only things that we can say we know for certain, are those things which we have personally experienced. In America there is a man who believes the earth is flat, so that if you keep going in one direction you will fall off, and he is ready to argue this belief with anyone. Some of his proofs seem quite strong. But I shall never argue with him, because I have had the experience of going directly westward from America and traveling in that same direction for many thousands of miles, and eventually coming back to the place I started from. So if that man argues until doomsday that the earth is flat and such a trip impossible, he cannot possibly convince me for I have made the trip. The same is true in regard to all sorts of knowledge. When experience speaks, doubt and uncertainty give way.

I recall an experience in my childhood when my father complained about a toothache; I could not understand why he should make such a fuss about one little tooth which could not hurt all that much. But some years later I woke up with a throbbing toothache that made it impossible to sleep. Then I understood why my father had complained so much about his toothache, and had no lingering doubt as to its intensity. Similarly I recall an experience when I first went to the city of Erivan in the Caucasus, and several people asked me whether I had yet seen Mt. Ararat. As it happened it was cloudy the day I arrived, and for several days afterward clouds hid the mountain from us. Having seen hundreds of mountains, I wondered why they all seemed so impressed with its beauty. Then one day the clouds dispersed and for the first time I saw that glorious towering mountain soaring 14,000 feet above the surrounding plain. Its peak was crowned with snow and glistening white clouds floated above it and I saw such beauty as I had not dreamed it could possess. For weeks after, the first thing every day I went out on the balcony to see whether Mt. Ararat was visible, and to refresh my soul with its extraordinary constantly changing beauty, and it has remained to this day as one of the most unforgettably lovely views to be found anywhere.

This same truth holds in regard to the beauty of music. I recall that when I was a small boy, classical music seemed to me something perfectly ridiculous. To me it was only a combination of meaningless noisy sounds. I would privately laugh at older people who claimed to find something beautiful in it and think they were just a group of snobs who pretended to enjoy it because it was the proper thing to do. But, as the years passed, the beauty of these same compositions began to grow on me until the time came when listening to their lovely melodies became one of my highest and purest joys, and the more I listen the more I find in them to admire. Just so is it with all spiritual sensations. The only conclusive proof comes with experience. My father could have argued endlessly to prove how hard a toothache is to endure without convincing me, but a half hour of experience proved it for all time. No matter how much my friends spoke in praise of the beauty of Mt. Ararat, their words had little effect—one clear sunny morning and all doubt was gone. And no matter how much my elders talked of the beauty of classical music, it was without effect until those sounds had created a response in my own soul and I began to enjoy them. And since knowing God is a type of learning, of wisdom, in this regard also the conclusive undeniable certainty comes from experience.

At this point we must pause to point out the difference between knowing about God and knowing God. Many have not realized this distinction and so do not get to the heart of the matter, but the difference is crucial. There is no one in America, for example, who has not heard of Abraham Lincoln, sixteenth president of the United States. We see his pictures in schools, in history books, on postage stamps and on coins. To some extent at least we are familiar with the highlights of his administration and his Emancipation Proclamation. From biographies we may learn much about his personal habits and abilities. But knowing all of these things does not make us personally acquainted with Abraham Lincoln. Since we were not in his presence, since we did not hear his voice or feel the impact of his personality, we cannot say that we knew him. We cannot claim such a privilege.

The same holds true for the knowledge of God. Knowing his qualities and his perfections does not constitute acquaintance with Him. We may feel that we understand thoroughly his laws and regulations, but still that does not constitute knowing Him. We may see every day the work of his hands and feel that we are witnessing revelations of his power and majesty of love. But this also is not knowing Him. So long as we have not heard his voice speaking in our hearts, have not felt the imprint of his personality and so long as we have not experienced the peace, joy, power and fellowship which He can give, we have no right to claim to know Him. But once we have had this experience, no one can convince us that there is no God. No further proofs and arguments are needed, and thereafter we speak of God whom we know.

Of course it is not possible to know everything about God. Indeed we cannot even know everything about ourselves. But we can know that which we need to know about God so as to be certain that God is living and to know what He wants us to do. But it is not easy to find this way. For there is just one way. Some think that in this respect all religions are alike so that it makes no difference which one of them one accepts as the purpose and goal of all is the same, i.e. to guide us to God. But the prophets themselves make no such claim. Moses constantly spoke on behalf of God and revealed God's laws to men. But he nowhere claims that men can come to know

God through him. Similarly David and Isaiah, and Jeremiah and every one of the Old Testament prophets made no such claim. According to an accepted tradition, Hazret-i Mohammed once said: "I do not know him (God) as I should." But Jesus' teaching is different. "I am the way. No one cometh unto the Father but by me" (John 14:6), and again, "No one knows the father but the Son and he to whom the Son reveals him" (Matthew 11:27). It is only Jesus who makes such a claim, and more importantly, makes the claim good.

Some may object to this and say "Why should this be so? Seeing that God is everywhere, why cannot we know him without an intermediary? Why should there be but one certain and particular way?" But this principle holds in regard to all universals. We can know them only by some particular embodiment. For example, it is impossible for us to understand exactly what time, in general, may be. But we can know limited portions of time, such as a second, a minute, a day or a year. We really know nothing of space in general, but we can know limited quantities of space such as centimeters, meters, kilometers, and circles. We know that water, in larger or smaller amounts, is to be found in practically everything; not merely in the rivers and oceans but in the sky, the air, the human body, in living plants and animals. But for the man who is thirsty this diffused moisture in everything is useless. If a traveler crossing the desert has no water aside from that diffused in the air and earth, he will die of thirst. Unless he reaches some well or spring where water is gathered in a usable quantity, he will surely perish. In the same way, God is everywhere and in everything. Yet unless one relates to Jesus, who is the water of life, his spiritual thirst will not be satisfied. In the same way, electricity, flowing electrons, can be found everywhere and in everything. Indeed everything is composed principally of electrons, the air, the water and the land. But all of these are quite useless to a man who wishes to light his electric lamp. He knows that unless he can find some electric outlet, all of this diffuse electricity is of no value to him. In the same way the power of God is everywhere present. It is to be found in all that exists. And there is one person through whom this power becomes available to us, and that is he who said: "Apart from me ye can do nothing" (John 15:5). Only by coming in touch with Him will our weak lamps be lighted, and the power of God flow into us and transform us. And that one person is Christ.

So how can one drink of this water of life and come in contact with this heavenly power? There are just two essential steps. As Jesus said: "Repent and believe on the Gospel" (Mark 1:15). First comes repentance, that is reversing the direction of our lives and turning away from sin. Our own experience, the Bible teaching, reason and logic—all teach us that there is one thing that cuts us off from God—and that one thing is sin. God is holy, and it is our sinfulness which separates us from God. God is a good God and He seeks the highest welfare of us all. It is our selfishness which estranges us from Him. He is a God of Love, and our hatreds are like a veil across his face, and hide Him from us. Therefore, the first requirement is that we separate ourselves from the sin that is a road block on the path to God. "If we confess our sin, He is faithful and just to forgive us our sin and to cleanse us from all unrighteousness" (I John 1:9). By means of confessing our sins in his presence, we pour out all the evil and corruption that is in us and permit his purity and cleanliness to take its place. Therefore, the first move on the way to God is to fall on our knees and confess to all the sin that is in us and turn from sin with complete resolution. Such confession is the first step on the way to God.

The second step is placing our trust in Christ. Trust does not simply mean that we give our mental approval to the statement that He is the world's Savior. Trust involves complete self surrender and submission, the surrender of our emotions and our wills to Him. Trust means complete confidence in Him who is our savior, who has made our salvation possible by his grace and love and sacrifice. And trust means unconditional acceptance of his commands for our daily life, complete surrender to his guidance and leadership for our lives and confidence in his power and ability to give us strength to carry out what He commands us to perform. Obedience is a word which many in this modern age dislike, as has been true in every age. But progress always depends on surrender to the facts. It is this way in the material world. People like to say that we have conquered nature and made it serve us in this twentieth century. But the exact opposite is the truth. The foundation for the progress we witness in our day, and its innumerable inventions, is laid on the discoveries made by scientists in the previous years of nature's laws, and in our learning to obey these laws and put them to work for meeting our needs. Before the automobile could become possible, it was necessary to understand the laws relative to electricity, dynamos, the battery, the electric spark. For the body of the machine, light and strong materials had to be discovered or developed. It was necessary to find methods of hardening rubber. It was necessary to discover and apply the laws of internal combustion engines to provide motive power. It was only after the discovery of all of these laws, and their application to every detail that it became possible for the automobile to be perfected.

In regard to religion also, growth and progress are only possible by obedience. Spiritual power is like electrical power in that only those who understand and comply with its laws can benefit from it. A good motive and desire are not sufficient apart from obedience to the laws. A small boy may set to work to build an automobile for himself, but in the absence of any knowledge of the laws by which it operates, his efforts will amount to nothing. Long before he is able to construct anything of value, his ignorance will bar him from making anything that resembles an automobile in any significant way. So it is not enough to have good intentions. In regard to God also, the same principles hold. However good and pure one's intentions may be—if he does not obey the laws which God has established and holy men have learned by the leading of His Spirit, he cannot succeed. Spiritual power will not be generated, unless the laws which God has laid down are obeyed—which requires repentance and confession of sin and surrender to Christ.

Here we will draw our discussion to a close. It is to be hoped that the readers who have read to this point may have found it fruitful, and may realize that not only is faith in God possible in this twentieth century, but that it is the most reasonable and logical belief that one may hold. More than that, we hope and pray that you may not merely come to a reasonable acceptance of the reality of God, but will follow the path of repentance and obedience so that you may know and experience the reality of God in your own life. "For this is life eternal that they should know thee the only true God and Jesus Christ whom thou hast sent" (John 17:3). We can assure you that if once you experience God and gain the peace and joy and growth which knowing Him imparts, you will look back on your present life and say with deepest appreciation: "I was dead and have come alive, I was lost and am found" (Luke 15:24).

ABOUT THE AUTHOR

John Elder (1894 -1981) was born in Tidioute, Penn. He received his B.A. degree, magna cum laude, from Washington and Jefferson College in 1915. In 1938 he was honored there with a D.D. degree.

Dr. Elder's first college interest was in the field of law. His decision was made in favor of the ministry, and he joined the Student Volunteer Movement. After teaching for one year, he began his studies at McCormick Theological Seminary.

When America entered the war in 1917, Dr. Elder went with 20 Y.M.C.A. secretaries to organize Y centers for soldiers in Russia. While they were crossing Siberia, the revolution began and Russian soldiers were going home. Some of the Y secretaries, unable to open Y centers as planned, returned home. Dr. Elder and one other young Y secretary took over responsibilities abandoned by relief workers fleeing the Turks in Armenia. They ultimately employed some 11,000 refugees and provided complete care for over 15,000 orphans, work finally backed by the Armenian Relief Committee.

In 1919 he returned to McCormick for a second year. Following this he became traveling secretary for the Student Volunteer Movement, combining full-time work with completion of his studies at McCormick in 1921-22.

In addition to the B.D. degree, McCormick awarded Dr. Elder the Bernadine Smith Orme Fellowship. This made it possible for him to take his bride, Ruth Roche (B.A. Wellesley, 1920) to Beirut, Lebanon, for a year to study Arabic—the language of the Koran. In 1923 they continued to their field of service, Iran, for evangelistic missionary work under the United Presbyterian Church-U.S.A.

They were assigned to Kermanshah, then to Hamadan, and finally to Teheran. Dr. Elder was successively pastor of the Persian-speaking congregation in each city. In 1935 he was Moderator of the Eastern Presbytery of Iran. He was Moderator of the Synod of Iran in 1947 and 1960. For 17 years he worked as secretary of the Inter-church Literature Committee in cooperation with the Anglican Mission.

In addition to his church-related responsibilities, Dr. Elder was from 1957 to 1964 a member and chairman of the Fulbright Committee and a member of the Eisenhower Scholarship committee for Iran. In 1957 he worked with Iran's Red Lion and Sun as co-director of flood relief. He was chairman of Earthquake Relief under the World Council of Churches, and helped rebuild a complete village, Esmatabad, which was destroyed in 1962.

At the conclusion of 42 years of service Dr. and Mrs. Elder moved to Ohio, where Dr. Elder served as supply pastor for several churches fairly near their home. Here he continued his scholarly interests, and when time permitted, enjoyed his six children and their families.

During the course of his work in Iran, Dr. Elder wrote numerous articles, pamphlets and books relating the message of the Bible to research and experience. These were published in Persian or English or, in some cases, both. His *Prophets, Idols and Diggers* was chosen in 1960 as a selection of the Religious Book of the Month Club. A number of his books have been translated into Arabic, Telegu and Portuguese. The present work, *Belief in God in the 20th Century,* was published originally in Persian. It is being published from the base English manuscript which Dr. Elder was revising before his death.

Titles of his published works, some of which are not yet published in English, include: *Topical Index of the Bible* (1935), *The Goodly Heritage* (1939), *History of the Reformation* (1947), *Path of Social Reform* (1951), *Science and Religion* (1953), *History of the Iran Mission* (1954), *Biblical Archeology* (1955), *Value of Religion to Society* (1955), *Prophets, Idols and Diggers,* published in England as *Archeology and the Bible* (1960), *Great Evangelists of Our Time* (1963), *History of the Christian Church from 600 A.D. to 1970 A.D.* (1971), and *The Biblical Approach to the Muslims* (1974).